WHO ARE YOU BEING?

By

U.R. CHOIX

Who Are You Being?
© 2020 U.R. Choix
All rights reserved.
For information, address: Attorney G. Payne at
gpayne@WiezorekPayne.com

ISBN (paperback): 978-1-7364527-0-7
ISBN (ebook): 978-1-7364527-1-4

Cover design: John Jalandoni

Printed in the United States of America

Paperback and ebook editions first published in January 2021

"*Who Are You Being?* is an important book that should be required reading for everyone at this time in our history. It emphasizes the value of the choices we make and their impact on the world at large. I highly recommend it."

—Jack Canfield
Coauthor of the #1 New York Times bestselling
Chicken Soup for the Soul ® series and *The Success Principles*™:
How to Get from Where You Are to Where You Want to Be

"*Who You Are Being?* is a unique read in that it integrates so many divergent wisdoms and perspectives from so many "big" thinkers — ancient and modern. *Who Are You Being?* offers practical tools to recognize where our power lies, and illuminates how to reclaim it, so we can live a life filled with joy, love, and peace. It's a welcome addition for elegantly surviving today."

—Jude Bijou, ma, mft
Author of *Attitude Reconstruction: A Blueprint for Building a Better Life*

"*Who Are You Being?* reminds us of our importance, that we are significant and that character matters. This book is a rare combination of common sense, deep insight, and smart, helpful guidance for all of us. Relevant and timely."

—T Harv Eker
#1 New York Times bestselling author of
Secrets of the Millionaire Mind™

"*Who Are You Being?* is a valuable guide for anyone who wants to access their inner power of choice to meet whatever life brings. It beckons us to recognize current changes and to lead positive change in our own lives and in our communities."

—Jill Morris
Coauthor of *Leadership Simple: Leading People
to Lead Themselves* and Cofounder of ChoiceWorks Inc.

AUTHOR'S NOTE

This book was written under the pseudonym U.R. Choix rather than the author's own name. It's important that the author be out of the way. This book is about you, the reader, and pulls together ideas and insights from some of the greatest minds out there.

Choix is French for choice. The name is meant to underscore that you are always at choice in your life. This book offers insights into the cultural forces impacting our lives today and the tools to discover who you want to be and who you are as you move forward. It is up to you how to interpret and use the ideas within these pages.

Wishing you a life's adventure filled with abundance and joy.

U.R. Choix

TABLE OF CONTENTS

Chapter One

WHERE WE ARE

Red or blue? Chances are that you interpret that question in political terms. Some of you may infer that I'm asking you to choose one color over the other. Today, it's more likely the question suggests an idea of us or them. Inherent divisiveness. Let's address the current political/social suggestion of this question. Within those three words are triggers for frustration, anxiety, stress, anger, and even depression. What happened to the notion that all people who consider America their home are US (not just U.S., but us)? This red versus blue stance, which is continuously fueled by the media and politicians, infects the culture. But, it's only one part of the problem.

We are a nation addicted to profit. One of the byproducts of this drive for the dollar has created countless disposable items instead of those we would take care of and use over and over again. Even expensive smart phones are encouraged to be replaced after a couple of years. In a culture where everything is disposable, we as citizens recognize, even if only on a subconscious level, that we are also disposable, especially if our "usefulness" has aged out. It's no surprise that a majority of our citizens do not feel heard, understood, or cared for. A growing aging population lives in fear of whether or not they can find a way to take care of their basic needs for the duration of what's left of their lives.

Do you find yourself increasingly anxious, frustrated, depressed, or angry even without one specific event triggering it? Or maybe you're seeing more and more people blaming everything and anything out in the world for their plight and turning to drugs or alcohol. Over the past decade, I've found myself curious about the kinds of changes I was seeing and experiencing. Initially, I wondered if this was unique to me; but over time and after speaking to countless others, I began to understand I wasn't alone. I am an avid reader and perpetual student, and throughout my life I have studied, in formal and informal ways, a variety of spiritual practices, personal growth philosophies, and cultural and historical human behavior. Over the past decade, I was driven to saturate our children with as much information as I could get my hands on, including bringing experts to the table in countless fields in a media series, where these experts could talk about their life lessons and experiences in those fields rather than simply the mechanics of the work itself.

I also began to notice the growing abdication of personal accountability in ordinary people, as well as in people who are in positions of power and influence. All you have to do is turn to the news in any form and you are assaulted with images and stories showing that we are in a time of bigotry, racism, public mud-slinging, mass shootings, bullying, one-upmanship, blaming, and suicide bombings. The current climate of divisiveness begs the question: how did we get here? It seems that not that long ago the climate was quite different, and our awareness as a nation about our need to come together to strengthen our future in light of climate change, globalization, and current issues that will affect that future was growing. What happened? In one way, the mask came off of what has been festering underneath and been repressed for decades. For most of us, the problem seems too big and we feel that we don't stand a chance in making a dent toward the solution.

I have felt growing anger, distrust, and judgment toward people I don't even know as a result of what I hear in the media or statements made out of context that put me into that same space of feeling 'it's us or them.' I have caught myself falling for the divisive rhetoric that's all around us. I have also had discussions with people who are the most loving, trusting, and inclusive people I can imagine, yet they too finally have come to a place of disgust and begin expressing things that are not inherently in their nature. All of this is destructive and unhealthy and something needs to change. When COVID-19 hit the world, I'd like to believe that it's the earth fighting for its own survival by forcing us all to shift toward an "us" mind frame. Unfortunately, the media and the current leadership have largely taken stances to further fuel the divide rather than work to bring us together.

How can an average person, whose daily priority is on survival, take the time and effort to be concerned with the decline of our culture? More importantly, how can we each possibly make a difference? In the most direct sense, individually we probably cannot make a huge dent, but in a very real scientific sense, we most certainly can. It's much like eating an elephant. One bite at a time. And that's where all of us, who are merely going about the business of living our lives and trying make the most and best out of those lives, come into play. We are experiencing fear and a culture of scarcity where we rarely feel like we are good enough, or that we continuously have to do more and overcome too many obstacles, or that we don't have enough in some way, especially when we repeatedly compare ourselves to those who superficially appear to be living the lives we feel should be ours. This fear and feeling of lack makes us turn on each other when that's the last thing we need to be doing. We need to find a way to come together.

I would argue that the root of why we have arrived at this place in our society is because, for most of us, our culture places little value on self-awareness, self-evaluation, introspection, going within, or however you choose to define the process of examining your own thoughts, emotions, reactions, actions, fears, and expectations; however, this is where change happens, where value can be found, and where character is grown.

Author Ekhart Tolle brilliantly explains in his book, *The Power of Now*, how "The quality of your consciousness at this moment is what shapes the future—which, of course, can only be experienced as the Now." Most anxiety, fear, frustration, anger, and perceived obstacles come from thinking about the kinds of experiences in our past or the perceived obstacles, attitudes, rejections, requirements, expectations of something in the future that we haven't yet experienced but that we are thinking about, fearing, or evaluating. Tolle explains that "Unease, anxiety, tension, stress, worry—all forms of fear—are caused by too much future, and not enough presence. Guilt, regret, resentment, grievances, sadness, bitterness, and all forms of non-forgiveness are caused by too much past, and not enough presence."

International lecturer, researcher, and author Dr. Joe Dispenza has successfully scientifically documented that what we do with each present moment is eminently creative and will result in our future.

Happiness, contentment, and satisfaction all come from within us. When you are present you can check within and monitor your inner state to gain more understanding and insight into yourself.

The present is all we really have—we really don't know what will happen in the next hour let alone next month or next year. Stories of lives changing in an instant are all around us. The COVID-19 pandemic changed the majority of our lives in ways we couldn't imagine. You can try to make your life as predictable and routine as possible, but are you striving for that false sense of security and comfort that comes from a perceived trust in outside forces? Or would you rather cultivate and develop a sense of comfort and peace within yourself no matter what is happening on the outside?

Imagine if each person simply focused on themselves and being the most and best they can be, what our country would begin to look like? I mean this in the form of the substance of "me," rather than the image or superficial aspects of "me" that we attempt to present to the outside world. Ours is a "me" culture where most of us think that what we do is only relevant as to how it impacts "me." What we fail to grasp is the enormity of how our actions ripple to others and theirs to us. A pandemic is a perfect example. If we stop comparing ourselves to everyone else, stop judging others and seeing certain people as enemies or obstacles, and stop focusing on outdoing someone else or putting them in their place, and instead put that energy into something positive and life affirming for ourselves and those we love, our lives will attract more happiness. I learned from author and personal coach T. Harv Ever, that what you focus on expands.

In *The Work* by Byron Katie, she offers that there are only three kinds of business: mine, yours, and God's (or the Universe's or whatever you consider as a "larger than us" concept). The idea is that if you are not minding your business, no one is at the helm of your life and you are at the greater mercy of outside forces. You need to stay in your own life's business rather than focusing your energy on one of the other two. Where your attention goes, energy flows and the results follow. For example, if you run a retail store, and instead of spending your time at the store, managing it, overseeing the books, analyzing your sales and getting familiar with your demographics and clients, you spend your time investigating the store across the street or complaining how they have long lines and extended outrageous hours with so many customers and building up your anger to the point that you miss certain facts—the fact that your own store is experiencing theft, slow-moving inventory, and other problems—then you wake-up one day and realize that your business has quickly evaporated. In effect, you have left your business unattended and the results show.

People who are too busy trying to figure out what another person is doing or gossiping about, or who are worried about their next move, are not looking at themselves and what they need to be tending to in their own lives. They become absent from taking care of themselves by spending so much time assuming they know what's going on with another person, and that person's motivations, intentions, and circumstances. There's a saying that "when you assume, you make an **ass** out of yo**u** and **me**." The truth is you can't know what it's like to be another person—not entirely and, even if you come close, chances are you will miss something along the way. Each one of us is as unique as a fingerprint. Making false assumptions has nothing to do with how smart, or not, you are.

If you have a family member, let's say a brother, who has experienced a tragedy and started drinking too much and you witness that his drinking has become a problem, what do you do?

Many of us are familiar with the concept of enabling. Enabling is one of the growing trends that has led to, as Greg Kukianoff and Jonathan Haidt call it in the title of their book, *The Coddling of the American Mind*, weakening rather than strengthening us.

Let's suppose that when your brother began his drinking you let it continue, believing that he was suffering. He wouldn't talk about it and would become defensive if anything were mentioned, so you didn't say anything. Secrets are a good substitute for boundaries. You continued to invite him to dinners despite his disruptive tendencies because he's your brother. Then he got a DUI and you bailed him out because he had no other family to help him. The saga continued until a great majority of your attention went toward being angry and dealing with your brother. Yet your brother continued being himself without acknowledging that he had any real problem or that his actions were affecting your family and you negatively.

When you are angry at someone, you give them your power. Then who's looking after you? What power do you have left to take care of your needs if you're giving the majority of your time, attention, and energy away?

The time to offer your brother your perspective on what you see and lay down some boundaries is as soon as you have the perspective and certainly when it begins to negatively affect your life. Some people find that action to be cruel; but without boundaries, we willingly give up the ability to positively grow our lives toward the vision we have for ourselves, and we take away our brother's opportunity to see what effect his actions have on others. Covering for people isn't always in the best interest of others, often quite to the contrary. The easier, less confrontational solution does not always serve the best interests of everyone involved. You are responsible only for your thoughts, your words, your deeds—not for anyone else's.

What is really within your control? You have no control over what another person thinks, feels, or does. You cannot control the weather, or the basic laws of physics, or time. What you can control is your reaction to every situation or obstacle, your thoughts, your attitude, and your actions. In your life, your responsibility is for the energy and the attitude that you bring to every situation and every space you occupy. You yourself are the only thing wholly under your control—what you say, what you do, and how you react to the world around you are a part of what defines you.

There's a story that you may have heard, but there is another takeaway from it other than the obvious. The story is about a woman standing on the side of an Alabama highway during a lashing rain storm. Her car had broken down (this was a time before cell phones) and she desperately needed a ride. Soaking wet, she attempted to flag down a car. Many passed her by, but a young white man stopped to help her. This was generally unheard of in the racially conflict-filled 1960s, as she was an African-American woman. The man took her to safety, helped her get assistance, and put her into a taxicab. The woman was calm, polite, and grateful, and although she seemed to be in a big hurry, she wrote down his address and thanked him. Seven days later, the man received a knock on his door and a console color TV was delivered to his home. The attached note read: "Thank you so much for assisting me on the highway the other night. The rain drenched not only my clothes, but also my spirits. Then you came along. Because of you, I was able to make it to my dying husband's bedside just before he passed away...God bless you for helping me and unselfishly serving another. Mrs. Nat King Cole."

How would you have reacted in her situation? Her husband was in the hospital dying. Her car broke down on her way to see him at night in a rainstorm. She was a black woman in the South during high racial tensions. These are factors she couldn't control.

Here is how she handled what she could control: She remained calm, assessed her options, took action to better her situation by flagging down a car (knowing that risk came with such an act), graciously explained her situation and accepted assistance, then she gave back to someone who helped her in a precarious situation. She could have been angry, agitated, frayed, and fearful, and that energy would likely have produced a different result.

It's not always easy to step back and stop yourself from being reactionary in a difficult situation. However, if you can create a habit of taking a deep breath and waiting a few moments before reacting in difficult situations, you might see the bigger picture and, as a result, adjust your actions and improve your outcome.

If we harnessed all the power (energy) we give away by being angry, analyzing other people's business, criticizing them and their actions, focusing on what they could do better, and instead applied that energy to furthering our desires, to asking ourselves where we need to go next, what steps we could take to get ourselves closer to our dreams, we would be a far more productive and happy people.

I believe that if we focus on being our best selves—in the sense of how we want to be treated; the kind of home, neighborhood, and family we want to be part of; and we start being that—we could indeed make a drastic difference to ourselves, our community, and our workplace. Once you start being that which you want to attract into your life, guess what? You start to attract just that into your life.

I witnessed a situation on a film set where a director became abusive. The production was a week away from completion when the director became irate and began behaving like a petulant child and then he became somewhat violent. The producer cleared the room and took the fight alone. The director was out of control and his behavior was beyond unacceptable. The producer could have justifiably fired him right then and there. The producer confided that common decency, ego, and anger really wanted her to go that way. Instead, she walked away, took many deep breaths and a few minutes to assess the situation and her options. If she were to fire him, production would have to stop, and not only would she need to find a replacement, the production would lose its location, much of the cast, and most likely would have had to start over. This option meant that everyone working on the film would lose both time and money and the project would not be completed, maybe ever. If she could come up with a compromise to placate him, then she could ensure that day's filming would be completed. Despite her desire to get rid of him, she found a way to restore peace. At the end of that day's work, the producer took the director aside and said that she was sure this was a singular incident and that he was not the kind of person who behaves this way, so let's put it behind us. Then she also warned him (in a non-threatening manner) to stay away from another such outburst or he would likely get reported to the Director's Guild. This way she could deal with the consequences of his behavior (and hold him accountable) after completing filming, which would serve the project and the most people in the long run. Her first commitment was to the project and those who depended on its completion without allowing or accepting destructive behavior while modeling sane, positive behavior.

This is not to say that when you first encounter difficult situations like this doing what would serve you and the greater good for the long run won't be hard. It might be very hard and you may want to throw in the towel. Just know that the first series of obstacles are the biggest tests. The beginning, when obstacles present themselves, is when your commitment is initially tested. If you keep re-affirming that commitment, the tests will keep coming but they will get easier to pass.

Reflections:

1. *What causes you fear, anxiety, and stress?*

2. *What makes you happy?*

3. *Do you find your thoughts focused mainly on the past, present, or*

the future? Where or on what do you expend most of your energy?

4. What would you like to change, do, or feel differently?

Chapter Two

WHERE TO BEGIN

Where do you begin? By taking a good look at yourself. Who are you being right now? What thoughts are you having? The reason for this last question is because the thoughts you have right now about yourself, your life, and your dreams are what will lead you to either act or not act, and those thoughts will determine your destiny. In the following chapters, I would like to help you explore those questions, along with some others, and bring one perspective that may be helpful. I would like you to start with taking a look at who you've been that has led you to who you are right now, examining the kind of person you are being, envisioning the kind of person you would like to be, then beginning the journey to be the best version of yourself that you wish to see.

Most young people growing up in contemporary American culture have, at some point in their early years, been asked, "What do you want to be when you grow up?" The focus is put on attaining a career label because most of us link our value with external markers of success, like money, status, and celebrity. What if we asked the question: Who do you want to be when you grow up? It may seem like a subtle difference, but in this question, there's a focus on your inner being, your humanity. It's a larger question that requires more thought and consideration of the whole of your life, not simply a discussion of what you will do for a living or a career. The who of yourself contains what kind of person you want to be as a friend, a contributor to society, a lover, a parent, a partner, a child, a sibling, an employee, a boss, and any other of the many relational structures you may be in.

From early civilization, one of the greatest (and briefest) teachings is from Plato—"Know thyself." The greatest power you have is to conquer yourself. This takes real courage; it requires facing and conquering your greatest fears. This is real power. A desire to have power over others when you don't have power over yourself stems from fear and this is a cowardly reach. The desire and need for the approval of others over being true to yourself is a road to disappointment.

When people make a positive mark on the world and affect others most profoundly, they stand for something meaningful. These are the people around you who stand for justice and truth. They choose integrity over their own comfort. They care for others, have compassion, kindness, humility, and a conscience—an ethical compass. They are people like the pharmaceutical representative who loses his job when he speaks up about one of the company's drugs that has a large percentage of fatal consequences. People like Colin Kaepernick, who was blackballed by the NFL because he dared to take a knee and make a statement for free speech and social justice. Whether you agree with them or not, these are the people we remember. We remember and are affected by these people not necessarily for what they have accomplished, but for who they are. People who have achieved inner integration and are not blown off course by life's storms. Their minds are stable and their hearts dependable and they don't need to prove anything to the world. Some historical and other examples are people such as Gandhi, Abraham Lincoln, Martin Luther King, Jr., Joan of Arc, Susan B. Anthony, Helen Keller, Eleanor Roosevelt, Nelson Mandela, and Ruth Bader Ginsberg.

I have followed the career of a young woman named Tiffany Shlain for the past decade. She began by making "cloud" films (those films made collaboratively with people all over the world, where individuals contribute their pieces, recorded on their cell phones, which are then edited together to make a cohesive film) around complicated subjects designed to ignite conversation. She began with one film at a time and over the years succeeded in engaging over fifty million people in dialogue, reaching embassies, governments, and ordinary people of all classes. She is an Emmy-nominated filmmaker and has received many awards and distinctions. In 2014 Shlain, along with her team at Let It Ripple, founded Character Day that quickly turned into a global movement where, once a year, millions of people all around the world engage in conversation and action around the idea of character. This movement is growing and informs us that we are hungry for validation and priority of inner values. People crave connection and, in the long run, it is more fulfilling than showing off a new toy.

The above-mentioned individuals are people of strong character. They possess integrity, strength, and fortitude of moral values. As writer Jim Loehr points out in his book, *The Only Way to*

Win: How Building Character Drives Higher Achievement and Greater Fulfillment In Business and Life, people of ethical character experience feelings of worthiness, fulfillment, and well-being. In a nutshell, they tend to be happier. Society has established our scorecard for how we measure success—money, status, power, and beauty. This scorecard affects all of us in how we validate our sense of self-worth and how we choose what and where to put our energy and time. In a society so focused on this type of scoring system, we can easily find ourselves chained to goals we think we should have rather than those that speak to our hearts. Living a life that's true to yourself, not the life others expect of you, requires strength of character. Character is not performance based (winning the gold medal, being President, writing a best-seller), it's morally based.

Legality is not a guide for morality. Because a thing may be legal does not necessarily make it moral. As history has shown, it is not okay to use a legal measure to defend the indefensible. Slavery, the Holocaust, wife beating, and burning people at the stake were all legal at one time.

So, how are we to build character in a landscape where we are bombarded with references to how we are controlled by culture versus how we are the ones to define it? As with all things, it begins within each of us. Your character is significant to who you are. It's your job to build your character. It doesn't happen by itself.

Your thoughts lead to intention. Your intentions lead to your actions. Your actions cause events and reactions that lead to habits. Your habits lead to your character and your character determines your destiny.

Thoughts > Intention > Actions > Events/Reactions > Habits

Our mainstream culture increasingly displays a lack of concrete moral vocabulary, leaving its people without an understanding of how to have an abundant inner life with any depth. The consequence of focusing on peoples' image, rather than on their inner core, distances us from what we value most.

When you encounter someone of great character, you cannot help being inspired or awed. There is an inner strength and peace that comes through them, and for a moment, you consciously or unconsciously want to bend your life to mimic theirs. Caring, wise hearts are obtained through lifetimes of diligent effort. They dig deeply within and heal lifetimes of scars. You can't teach character or email it or tweet it. It has to be discovered within the depths of your own heart when you are finally ready to go looking for it. The job of a wise person is to swallow the frustration and go on setting an example of caring and cultivating and diligence in their own lives. What a wise person teaches is only the smallest part of what they give. The totality of their life, of the way they go about living their life in the smallest details, is what gets passed on.

Think about your essence. The person you identify yourself as being. The person you want to be remembered as and the one you are proudest of. Embody that in mind and heart and your actions will follow. Don't confuse people of character with those of fame and wealth. William Randolph Hearst is considered "a character" who is noteworthy because of his vast publishing empire. If, however, you dig a little deeper, you learn that his empire was inherited from his father, then built up through less than honest and honorable practices, and often through an abuse of power. It is believed that he hated minorities and used his chain of newspapers to inflame racial tensions at every opportunity. While married, he had an ongoing affair with actress Marion Davies. His hypocrisy was apparent in that he and Ms. Davies shared a bed, but he wouldn't allow any of his guests to have a companion out of wedlock and he vehemently judged and spoke out against people who did exactly what he did. Although renown, he was not a man of character.

Why are so many wealthy people inwardly unfulfilled when they can have (superficially) anything they want? In our society it is common to be torn between the person who wants to excel at a career at any cost and the person who wants to develop and uphold a strong moral core while also excelling. Excelling in your career focuses on outward performance, which can easily neglect your moral compass. We've been taught to judge others by outwardly recognized achievements, the appearance of their abilities, as well as their physical appearance. We are told to promote and advertise ourselves and to master the skills required for monetary success and to continue to further a consumer culture. We encourage creating and projecting our brand, our image. We teach and preach how to promote ourselves as a product and how to promote whatever product we want to sell, and how to consume more and more, rather than to promote the core values that can sustain us. What we tend not to encourage is humility, sympathy, and honest self-evaluation, which are all essential to building character.

We are influenced to satisfy our desires and material drives and we lose sight of the moral stakes involved in every day decisions. I was witness to an incident where two board members of a Home

Owners Association secretly, and without board approval, caused the cutting down of dozens of mature trees in the community, falsely claiming it was necessary because of some made-up reason. They did this because they wanted only one specific type of tree and believed they could force the developer to pay for these replacements. One of the trees was a decade old and provided the majority of shade for the main parking lot. However, this tree blocked a part of the view of the mountains from the main board member's home. Unbeknownst to other board members, he was putting his home up for sale and wanted to claim an unobstructed view in his marketing materials. The community lost these trees, had to replace them at its own expense, and replaced them with the same trees that were taken down. When the board member's home went up for sale, the new owners preferred the same type of tree to be put back where the original one was because it created both a sound barrier as well as beauty and shade, but now it would take years to mature. The board member acted out of greed over integrity and the community lost not only money but the mature trees that they valued, which would take years to flourish again.

We are responsible in cultivating our inner lives on our own. We cannot expect of others what we are unwilling to do ourselves. Without a satisfying inner life, happiness is only fleeting. A deep sense of contentment comes from inner richness. Be willing to really look at yourself and confront the why of what you're doing and, in so doing, you have a chance at building stronger character and virtue and leaving a legacy that lives on in people's hearts. "The line separating good and evil passes not through states, nor between classes, nor between political parties either—but right through every human heart," said author Aleksandr Solzehenitsyn.

The virtues among those of strong character are the maturing virtues of those who have lived fully and have learned from joy and pain. They have not led conflict-free lives, rather they have struggled toward maturity and wisdom. These are people who get things done without the need to showboat their achievements. The life of John McCain is such an example. People with wise hearts move with ease through different social classes and you don't see them being self-righteous.

Character begins within. Deepening of character begins with the willingness to look within and then doing some inner evaluation.

Our younger generations have an unprecedented level of self-infatuation. This was revealed in a recent analysis of the American Freshman Survey, which has been asking students to rate themselves compared to their peers since 1966. Psychologist Jean Twenge and her colleagues compiled the data and found that over the last four decades (beginning in the late 1970s) there has been a dramatic rise in the number of students who describe themselves as being 'above average' in the areas of academic ability, drive to achieve, mathematical ability, and self- confidence. However, researchers found a disconnect between the student's opinions of themselves and their actual abilities. They thought they were more talented and capable than they actually were. In appraising the traits that are considered less individualistic—co-operativeness, understanding others, and spirituality—the numbers either stayed at or slightly decreased over the same period.

In the last twenty-five years or so, the practice of giving children awards for everything starting from when they're in preschool and continuing through college has increased exponentially. Awards for attendance (seriously? Isn't this a requirement rather than a talent?), for participation (again, why are you here if you aren't supposed to participate?), and a myriad of other ridiculous certificates and awards given without a basis on real merit or exceptionalism. There is a fine line between building healthy self-esteem in our children and in each other and that of creating an over-inflated sense of self and an unjustified sense of grandeur. Renowned psychologist Jim Loehr reminds us that "any self esteem, high or low, that is contingent on something beyond one's control breaks easily." There is no connection between self-esteem and character. You can have high self-esteem and be lacking in character and vice versa.

While the Twenge study focused on the younger generation, other studies have shown that as a culture overall, no matter your age, this sense of self-importance and entitlement has substantially increased within the population. The median narcissism score has risen 30 percent in the last two decades. Social media image-based forums are one of the culprits. These are cyber places where anyone can post anything and create the way they want to be perceived—regardless of reality. This creation can become a mechanism for self-delusion. Whatever the cause or whatever you want to call it, something is happening within our culture and it is cause for examination because a problematic shift is afoot.

Looking at history, the reactions, behaviors, and values of previous generations hold some wisdom. This is not to say that we want to mirror the culture of previous times, because in many ways we have progressed and advanced. However, we should take a look and see if we lost something in the process. For example, in David

Brooks' book *The Road to Character*, he describes a program he heard on NPR's "Command Performance" that was broadcast to the U.S. troops near the end of WWII, when the Allies had just completed one of the most significant military victories in history. The tone of the program was one of humility despite the great victory. "We won this war because our men are brave and because of many other things—because Russia, England, and China and the passage of time and the gift of nature's materials. We did not win it because destiny created us better than all other people. I hope that in victory we are more grateful than proud." Brooks says, "The show mirrored the reaction of the nation at large...This was in part because the war had been such an epochal event, and had produced such rivers of blood, that individuals felt small in comparison...People around the world had just seen the savagery human beings are capable of...The knowledge of victory was as charged with sorrow and doubt as with joy and gratitude...their first instinct was to remind themselves they were not morally superior to anyone else."

Brooks then goes on to say that after listening to that program he turned on a football game and "A quarterback threw a short pass to a wide receiver, who was tackled almost immediately for a two-yard gain. The defensive player did what all professional athletes do these days in moments of personal accomplishment. He did a self-puffing victory dance as the camera lingered. It occurred to me that I had just watched more self-celebration after a two-yard gain than I had heard after the United States won World War II. It occurred to me that this shift might symbolize a shift in culture, a shift from a culture of self-effacement that says, 'Nobody's better than me, but I'm no better than anyone else' to a culture of self-promotion that says 'Recognize my accomplishments, I'm pretty special'."

When we tout our every accomplishment—such as 'I lost twenty pounds,' 'I worked out four times this week,' 'I cleaned my closet,' 'My YouTube view got 5000 hits,'—and scream about how special we are, then it becomes much harder to witness and appreciate true accomplishment, real heroes, and something uniquely special. The special gets lost in the noise of the mundane. As more and more people add their voice and try to become louder than everyone else, the noise simply increases. Fame is not a talent nor a virtue nor a real accomplishment, yet fifty-one percent of young people say being famous is one of their top personal goals.

Our desire for instant gratification is diminishing the reverence for true accomplishment made by learning, practice, experience, and honing and maturing talent over time. Character is built through thought, observation (both self and others), being discriminate and open-minded, curiosity, live interaction, and experience.

Character essence holds a self-effacing quality that is soothing and gracious, while the self-promoting person feeds his/her ego. Egotism is self-concerned, competitive, and distinction hungry, while humility is infused with admiration, companionship, and gratitude. When you embody that kind of humility, you are unable to ignore your own ignorance. You realize that there's a lot you don't know and that a lot of what you do know may be distorted or incorrect. This is how humility leads to wisdom. The admired strive to magnify what is best in themselves, to defeat what is worst, and to become strong in the places they are weak. They are aware of the flaws in their own nature. I invite you to begin your own self exploration.

Why begin with you? Because as actor Mark Lewis points out, "The person who you're with most in life is yourself and if you don't like yourself you're always with somebody you don't like."

What's Your Story

Your story consists of events of your past, your history/herstory, and your interpretation of and reactions to those events. These have shaped you. Your history is the foundation of your story and you. It has brought you to where you are today. Give your history respect for getting you here. If you are reading this book, your story has brought you to a place of curiosity.

Your story is more complicated than just your past. This is where you put meaning and emotion into that past. This is where choice and destiny come into play. Within your story is the question of how you address and accept who you are and where you come from with where you want to go and who you want to be.

If I'm going to ask you to consider your story, I think it's only fair that as the author, I also tell you some of my story as is relevant to the writing of this book. I have lived and traveled all over the world, and I love this planet. I have lived within several cultures, speak several languages, and have observed that our humanity shares a common thread where our inner similarities (our desires, our concerns, and our fears) far outweigh our differences. Today, our connections as a human race are more vast and far reaching than ever before. The United States is my home and as such my focus is primarily on our culture and that of Western society, because we are the largest and loudest voice in terms of economics and leadership.

Therefore, I think it's fair that we begin with ourselves.

I have been writing in some form all of my life. I wrote my first book when I was seven years old, complete with felt cut-out illustrations much to the delight of my second grade teacher. I have had some success and some failure and, like most writers, much frustration along the way—each a growth experience. The media series that I mentioned in the first chapter compelled me to begin writing about my thoughts on what I was hearing not only from the experts but from the young people I found myself surrounded by. In addition to that desire for mentorship, a series of events led me to finally sit down and begin writing what's been on my mind for years. Condensed, those events boil down to the following:

One, when my lunch companion (a college-educated, professional man in his forties) expressed genuine sincerity when he said he never thought to consider a value greater than money, I suggested that perhaps life should be placed as a value greater than money, because money without life, without a life to enjoy or share or breathe or eat, has no value. He thought for a moment and said, "Yes. Wow. I never thought of that." I was stunned, not only for the common sense reason, but because over the past decades that is what we've come to believe as our highest value—money. I looked up some statistics and discovered that for ten million dollars most Americans would abandon their families, their friends, and their church. And a small, but not insignificant, percentage would consider changing their race, their sex, and even consider committing murder.

Two, after the 2016 Presidential election, I watched a woman being interviewed on the news. The reporter asked her if she were still going to vote for the man who spoke in such a demeaning manner about women and grabbing their "pussies." She said, "Sure. Men say stuff like that all the time. They always trash on women. I've heard worse." She said that as an explanation of why it's okay to vote for a man who is publicly demeaning and abusive to women, because in her experience men like that are normal. To approve of this and call it normal sent me to question how we got here. How any woman could be there, let alone so many women.

Three, the news. From coverage of leaders saying things like in case of "legitimate rape" a "woman's body would shut down and not get pregnant" to the media's continuous coverage of opinions—even if they were blatant lies—as news and worthy of discussion to mass shootings after which numerous leaders advocated for even more guns, all revealed a media focused on sensationalism rather than facts and educating their citizens.

Four, my own reactions, which I mentioned at the beginning of this book.

Five, the outbreak of the Coronavirus and the leadership minimizing and blaming political opponents, people like Alex Jones selling sham remedies, and those who hoard supplies then attempt to sell them at unconscionably inflated prices. In addition to the negative spin I mentioned, this outbreak is evolving and many positive elements of human behavior are afoot, which I hope will be highlighted in the media and a move toward actual journalism rather than sensationalism will begin.

Six, the murder of several Black Americans at the hands of police that led to protests around the world. The peaceful protests were commendable, while the violence and riots were troubling. An element that concerned me is the divisive language used by some protestors as well as some media personalities on all sides. The protesters were quick to banish someone's comment if they didn't use a correct word or attribution, even if that person was supportive of their cause, such as Ellen DeGeneres. Ellen said, "People of color in this country have faced injustice for far too long. For things to change, things must change. We must commit ourselves to this change with conviction and love." She was harshly criticized for saying 'people of color'. This led to others remaining silent for fear of similar backlash.

I wanted to try and understand the underlying reasons for how we got here, what's missing, and what we can do to elevate the connections of our lives.

When you are asked, "What's your story?," you can choose the things you want to mention. Where you're from, your education, relationships, work, family history, and the events that you feel have shaped you. We tend to think our story is merely about the facts of our past, but as I mentioned, there's more to it than that. In your choices of what to relay, you reveal what you value. Your story lies in what you pull out of your background and how you choose to interpret those events in your life. What elements are you choosing from your past to define you? Write down your story as you think about it.

In your narrative lies the influential seeds that affect the big picture of who you will become and who you have been up to this point. How you interpret the roots of your past ultimately shapes your life. Clinging to certain elements of your story creates certain patterns in your life. Some examples of those patterns might be your ability or inability to take action, to make decisions, to accept responsibility, to disengage from blame, or to be distrustful in how you relate to others.

If your story ties you to a vision of yourself as needing to stay small and to not speak up; or feeling as if you have to know everything and have to always be right to not be considered weak; or that you were born to struggle and life is hard; or that good things don't come easily for you; or any number of other limiting beliefs, then your story limits you as you go through life, and my bet is that it prevents you from being who you really want to be.

For example, a teenage boy came home from school one day and discovered that his family's home burned to the ground right after his father left them. His story became one of abandonment and loss. As the years passed, he attracted relationships in which his partners left him. Their leaving reinforced his story. He expected it. He also discovered that anytime he received something big or good, he would lose it. He was not surprised by this either, fully expecting more loss. In his mind, life brought abandonment and loss, and the universe delivered to him his expectations.

Another teenage boy had the same set of circumstances. His father left the family a few weeks before their home was consumed by fire and they had to find another place to live and they had to recreate their life. His story became one of finding a new path out of tragedy. As the years passed, he found himself living in new cities, up-leveling his circumstances at every turn, and finding people he could count on so that he could eventually provide for his own family and his mother in a way his father never did.

In having their home burn to the ground and a parent leave,

one man chose to carry his loss forward throughout his life and to re-create the elements of tragedy, while the other one chose to recognize the loss and add to his story that it was a way to make him stronger and take him to a new home and discard the destructive elements of behavior he saw in his father.

Neither one is right or wrong. It is merely a choice. Sometimes realizing that we have the power to make such a choice can fill us with trepidation, fear, and anxiety, because the power lies within you and not out there. In her book *Becoming,* former First Lady Michelle Obama points out that "failure is a feeling long before it's an actual result." The only question you need to ask yourself is—Does the story you're telling yourself serve you in who you want to be? Much like where you place your attention is where you place your energy, the parts of your life you select as your story become your identity.

Consider Your Story:

1. What do you do for a living? Are you proud of the work that you do? Why or why not?

2. What types of thoughts preoccupy you? Your problems? Your hurts or betrayals? Do you easily judge others?

3. List three events that have defined your outlook on life.

4. What parts of your story do you tell that give you strength? What parts make you feel weak?

5. How can you reframe the parts of your story you don't like into parts that you do?

Chapter Three

DEFINING WHO YOU ARE BEING NOW

The World Is Your Mirror

Look at yourself first. Most of us look first for who or what we can blame, rather than looking at our part in events when something goes wrong. In the narrative of your story, do you place blame on others and on circumstances? Be honest with yourself. Do you own up to a mistake when you make it? Do you make decisions, right or wrong, when necessary, or do you delay until it's too late? If you don't know what to do, do you ask for help or do the research to find out, or do you throw up your hands and wait for someone else to do it? Do you go after what you want, trying different avenues, or do you lament because what you want isn't being handed to you? Are you a problem solver or a complainer? Do you ever look around and wonder why you find yourself in certain circumstances again and again? Or why you tend to attract certain types of people into your life? Consider this: Your thoughts are the seeds in creating your life. The next layer is your word: what you say is a reflection of who you are. If your words don't match your thoughts, the first link in the chain to creating what you want to create is broken. Next, if your words don't match your actions, the next link is broken and success in manifesting your visions becomes that much more difficult. In examining your story, it helps to look at the life you've created.

The notion that your inner world creates and is reflected back to you by your outer world can be frightening. Physicist Brian Green explains how everything in our universe is connected and interdependent, including your thoughts and how they affect the dynamics of your life, which might give you some insight into how this can work since your thoughts are vibrations. Those vibrations link to an unseen web of vibrations emanating from everyone else and connect us all. If you are interested in the science of this unifying force, look up Mr. Green along with the science of super string theory. Knowing that by changing your inner self (your beliefs, your thoughts, your perspective) you can change your individual world can be a comfort. Accept the power that your thoughts have on your life.

Saying that the world is your mirror refers to your ability to manifest. Your thoughts are creative. Your thoughts lead to feelings that lead to actions that then lead to results. The world reflects back to you, much like a mirror, what your inner landscape has been creating. Our larger world is a collective manifestation. Within that collective world are our individual worlds—our particular reality and our unique life experience. There are as many realities as there are people.

You create your life as you go along; therefore, your experiences can give you an instant and ongoing reflection of who you are. Using your external world as your mirror and learning how to perceive and interpret its reflection can help you see your beliefs, attitudes, and emotional patterns. You can uncover hidden aspects of yourself that you may not wish to see or acknowledge otherwise. By seeing the reflection or result of your inner workings, you can work backwards as to how it may have come about and what you may wish to shift or change.

An example might be the woman nearing forty who says she wants a baby, but despite her long-term committed relationship and no fertility issues has always found an excuse why the timing to try was always wrong. She thinks she's finally ready and goes to the doctor for an in-vitro procedure, only to discover that she has a benign tumor that must be removed first. After that, she thinks she should wait some more and before she knows it, it's too late. When she takes apart her history she discovers that when opportunities to incorporate or even tolerate children in her life presented themselves, something else also became apparent: her need to be able to fully control her immediate world and surroundings. She saw this through a series of events: when she and her husband agreed on a timeline, she found a reason to postpone the first time again and again to the point where he finally left her; when her sister and niece came to stay and her niece got the flu, she asked them to leave for fear of getting sick; when her friends came over with toddlers, she would insist they all go to the park to avoid creating a mess in her house and then discovered that she found a way to not have them over again. She enjoyed children in small doses on her terms, but the unpredictability of a child left her panicked and lost.

I believe that you attract the people and circumstances of your life. If they create problems or struggles for you, this isn't a call to put yourself down, rather it's a call to identify a signal of where to look inside for healing, awareness, focus, or unhealthy beliefs. This would be the time to ask yourself questions such as: Do I trust myself? What am I really afraid of? What do I believe about myself or about what is possible? Do I feel hopeless? Why? How could I feel inspired and strong? What do I believe about this thing that isn't working? If I see that I am consistently jobless, but I say I believe that I deserve and can do a great job, then what's missing? Dissect those beliefs in full view of the reflection you see.

Spiritual leader Gangaji writes that "...your life as you live it now is the reflection of what you really want. If what you really want is truth, then you will live in surrender to that and not in surrender to phenomenal display. Whether it is the phenomenon of personal power, or sexual excitement, or spiritual power, it is all a trap of the mind."

You may have heard the story about a small town that flooded. The flooding was so great that it began to envelop all the houses in the vicinity. Some people created whatever they could find to make rafts. Others bonded together and swam to assistance. One man, a deeply religious man, believed that God would save him and so he stayed put as his house filled with water. The emergency crews were supplied with boats and began going around picking up anyone who was stuck. When they came upon the stranded man, he waved them off and said he was fine, that God would save him. When the water got so deep that it came up to the roof of the house, the man climbed up on his roof and waited. A rescue helicopter came by and dropped him a line, but he refused it, saying that God would save him. Soon the entire house was engulfed in water. The man struggled to swim and shook his fist up at God yelling, "Why did you do this to me? You were supposed to save me!" and God replied, "I gave you enough warning, but you stayed and did nothing, then I sent you a boat, but you shooed them away. Finally I sent you a helicopter, but you wouldn't get in."

Keep an open mind about what you see in your life and what it may indicate about your personal story. Loosen up any rigidity toward what you think a solution to a particular problem has to look like and you may discover that it has been there all along, you simply needed to adjust your perspective.

Are You A Coward?

The definition of a coward is a person who lacks the courage to do or endure dangerous or unpleasant things or one who is excessively afraid of danger or pain. Notice that being a coward is not just being afraid of something dangerous or life threatening. The definition includes "unpleasant" things and being excessively afraid of pain. Looking at the statistics of alcoholism, obesity, opiate and pain killer addiction in the U.S., I would offer that a great many of us are excessively afraid of pain and looking to anesthetize our way out. The definition doesn't say a person who isn't afraid or doesn't feel fear. Many of the bravest people feel the most intense fear. What makes them brave rather than cowardly is that they act in spite of that fear. Fear is a natural phenomena and some fear is healthy while some is self-imposed and merely a construct of our thoughts used to debilitate and keep us in our comfort zone.

When you see a wrong being perpetrated, do you speak up

and/or do something or do you turn away? How many times do you hear of an act of violence taking place in a public place with many people around, but no one steps forward to do anything? What's worse is that sometimes not even one person can be found to speak up about what they saw as a witness. There are instances when you may feel your life would be in danger if you spoke up and it may be true, especially if you were alone. However, in the example above, if several people were willing to come forward, then the danger would significantly decrease and wrongs would be righted more readily. There is power in numbers on every scale. Unfortunately, in today's society, the numbers of cowards seems to outnumber the few brave souls out there. I say this based on personal experience as well as evidence within the media and what I see in all forms of news, such as the continuous accounts of politicians or corporate leaders holding a particular position one day, then claiming they never said it the next, or one political party blaming the other and tearing down people rather than moving toward solutions, or name calling and blaming coming from people who hold high positions of power, including the Presidency, and very few members of the press coming forward with strong, bold statements of truth fearing reprisal. I invite you to change those numbers.

Courage begins with small individual acts. It begins with you. It begins with being undaunted within and acknowledging your fears, your biases, your strengths, and your weaknesses. Second, courage requires you to confront those things within you that need to be confronted and overcome for you to begin to embody the highest vision for yourself.

If you say you believe in something, but when confronted with the most dire and challenging of circumstances you act contrary to that belief, then your word and your being becomes untrustworthy and loses its power. It is during those times that you truly discover who you are and can decide who you want to be. Every action you take, every action you do not take, speaks to who you are.

Some examples to think about: 1) The people who claim to be pro-life (really meant to be against a woman's right to choose) yet blow up abortion clinics causing deaths. I've asked some people what they mean by pro-life and they say that to them every life is important and has the right to be and they believe that life begins at conception. Those same people typically vote for the death penalty. Some of those people that I know also advocate for more guns and lax gun laws and yet they stand by and watch children being shot in schools, theaters, and clubs, year after year. If you say you believe in life, but are willing to take the life of another or to excuse another person who does, what does that say about either your belief or your word or both? 2) Those who are devout in a faith claim they believe in that faith because it is just, loving, and supports a higher human vision, yet those same faithful are intolerant of the humans who believe in something else that they too claim to be just, loving, and support a higher human vision. What does that say about their ability to actually be just, loving, and supporting a higher vision? 3) People from within the Michigan Department of Environmental Quality (MDEQ), other government agencies, and the State's Representatives in Flint, Michigan, were charged with protecting the interests of their community. Yet, despite numerous complaints and evidence of harmful water filled with lead, they decided to look the other way and allow the contamination all in an effort to save money. Those people threw their Flint community under the bus, then reframed the situation to keep the facts from their constituents and likely also reframed it in their own minds to assuage the guilt of allowing numerous children to die and numerous others to suffer from on-going health problems from heart issues to brain damage. Passing the buck from person to person and agency to agency masks the truth. Such tactics can be supported only within a culture where people think those tactics are justifiable as long as you don't get caught. Such lies are the mark of a coward.

There are plenty of positions of power/decision-making authority that cowards hold. However, cowards are never true leaders because their flock consists of the fearful who are easily turned by more fear. Tyrants depend on cowards. If you admire someone in a position of high public office, management, or any position of greater authority, ask yourself if they are a leader or if they merely rely on the use of fear for their authority.

Some questions to consider when looking at your own inclinations:

* When you make a mistake, even a huge one, do you own up to it?
* If you have an opinion different than your boss, do you say so under circumstances where it will significantly affect something or someone?
* If you disagree with a prominent person in the room, do you go along or speak your mind? Do you blame them later by gossiping, and criticize them rather than speak up?
* Do you fall in line just because everyone else does and you're afraid to make a scene if you don't do the same

because you'd displease a powerful person?

* Do you prefer not knowing (ignorance) something if it would disturb your life?

* Will you defend someone you know is innocent if it threatens to ostracize you from your tribe, who might then accuse you of being on the wrong side?

Imagine what the world would be like if we changed the numbers and more people were willing to stand up and be brave rather than cower in fear.

Feeling Victimized?

As you think about your story, notice that nothing has any meaning except for the meaning you give it. If in your story you are complaining, blaming, criticizing, or comparing, then chances are that you are relaying to others your victimization in some way as part of your story. You are telling part of your story in a way that makes you appear to be a victim of your circumstances and events. You are relaying that events on the outside had "power" over you in some way. And you are carrying that victimization forward into your now.

Most people will argue that if they were wronged in some way, it's a fact. Some factual events are indisputable—e.g. being shot during a random act of violence, a wildfire that destroys your home, or an economic crash that changes the circumstances of what you have to work with. That may all be true; however, there is a difference between what happens to you and the choices you make pertaining to what happens. I believe that it's what you do with the actual underlying facts that counts. Let's say you were abandoned as a child and every time you tell your story, you relay how you were abandoned and how those scars are still with you and how they prevent you from being able to trust people. Every time you focus on the scarring nature of the abandonment, which may have taken place forty or more years ago, you reinforce the scar and, in your current reality, you are creating an inability to trust. Your past isn't creating that current reality for you. Your choice to focus on a disempowering perspective is what is creating it for you. What you are choosing is to remain in the emotional space of the fear of what abandonment feels like, rather than using your frontal lobe and making a conscious, thought out choice to disconnect from a past emotion from affecting and dictating your present circumstances and leaving it in the past—where it belongs. Consider a different perspective on the same underlying fact: Because I was abandoned as a child, I experienced and learned how to be self-reliant, how to read people and to follow my instincts. Sometimes the lessons were hard, but they led me to a greater understanding of what it takes for me to be able to trust and how to empower myself now in a way I could not as a child.

You can choose, in any given moment, the disempowering perspective or the empowering one. Focusing on events in a way that paint you as the victim constantly reinforces what is wrong in your life. It also reinforces what is wrong with everyone else around you, which is really a reflection of your inner angst. I'm not saying that if you've suffered a great tragedy or real wound that you don't need time or help to heal from it. You do. Denial and repression get you nowhere. I encourage you to take your healing seriously. Grieve, accept, incorporate, then find the best way to move on. However, just as repressing your need for healing won't get you anywhere, neither will wallowing in your woundology. When you live in the anxiety and suffering of what happened to you or didn't happen, you are negatively affecting your own life as well as the lives of those around you. Your suffering affects the people who love you and work with you, sometimes directly in physical interaction and other times more energetically.

I'm not saying it's easy to let the disempowering focus go, nor am I saying that those thoughts won't slip in from time to time. I am saying that if you don't want them to control your life, you can make a different choice and do your best to stick with it. It's worth trying. Think about what it would be worth for you to change your perspective about your history.

Let's talk about how focusing on something—be it an idea, a hurt, a wrong, a situation, or an unfulfilled desire—even if only a little, but doing it repeatedly, grows that thing in your life. What you focus on expands.

When you are immersed in a project and focusing on completing it, all of your thoughts and actions are flowing toward that end. Your focus is on finishing it and when you do, it is a gratifying experience. When you focus on creating an event, for example, a dinner party, you devote the mental and physical time and energy toward it and make it happen. So it is with all of the things we need and want. I've heard people say, "I long to be in a great love relationship, but I wonder if it even exists. If it does, it's rare." That person is likely focused on the longing and the rarity of that type of relationship and so they attract more longing and rarity in that area. Whatever you believe and focus on will be the thing that expands in your life. If you are unhappy and focus on what is bringing you discontent, you will only grow more of that and bring in more unhappiness since you are growing it with your focus along with the emotions and vibrations that go with it.

Many people believe in the power of mantras, or sayings, that they repeat daily, believing that saying something over and over can help it come true. It can work if their thoughts and beliefs support what they are saying. Our thoughts and beliefs in large part create our personal world. How you see something is how it ultimately becomes. If you look at a flower and find it beautiful, and you are given that flower by someone you like, then the association for you is positive. But, if that same flower is one you find ugly and it is given to you by the same person, chances are you will not have the same reaction, you might be suspicious or see that person differently or whatever else you choose to conjure. Conversely, if a person you dislike gives you your favorite flower, you may suddenly have more positive feelings toward them. You choose the way you see a thing. Remember, it has no meaning except the one you give it. Much like the Rorschach cards—they are what the person looking at them sees and nothing more or less. Ten people can watch the same video of an event and give ten different perspectives on that same event. A perfect example is a football or basketball game when there's a play or a foul that the referee calls one way but some fans and some players see it another and replays are examined and discussed. Where your focus goes your reality follows.

If you feel victimized, you focus on your pain and how you have been wronged. That focus keeps you busy and allows you to avoid looking at your inner life. You can't see any issues you have been avoiding because avoiding your pain takes priority. But, masking your pain doesn't get to the root of it or allow you to expel that root once and for all. You are not alone.

We are a nation in pain and the ways that our culture masks this pain is through drug use (both prescription and illegal), alcohol abuse, and overeating. The why of this is multi-layered and no one has come up with a clear and undisputed answer. I would like to propose that one of the elements that has fostered and grown our pain can be found in our collective subconscious. That element is that as a culture we do not take care of each other. It's every person for themselves. As a nation, we place profit above the health of our people, above our mental and emotional well-being as a society (consider the closing of the nation's mental institutions to save money, which has now produced countless homeless persons costing us even more), and our hunger for more and more profit takes away from the areas of healthful food, health care, clean water and air, healthy soil and nature, and taking care of and educating our children. Some of our "foods" cause cancer and yet they are put in our schools, and there are too many places where drinking water is allowed to remain toxic and insurance companies fight to reject health needs. As a culture, we don't do well with the vulnerable and many find shame in being vulnerable because of the stigma. On a subconscious level, we all know that, as a culture, we do not tolerate most vulnerabilities for very long and if we *are* vulnerable we are not cared for. Compound this with a situation where you feel isolated or your personal circumstances hit a snag, and it's that much easier to go down a rabbit hole. When something terrible or jarring happens in our personal lives, we are not supported by our culture. If you are fortunate, you have a strong family and friend support system that will prioritize caring for you if you should become vulnerable. But how effective can they be if the rest of our culture isn't there to back us up?

I say this because of the unavoidable statistics on these topics. Let's start with drug use. According to the National Institute on Drug Abuse, every day in the U.S., 2,500 youth (ages 12 to 17) abuse a prescription pain reliever for the first time. The National Center for Health Statistics at the Center for Disease Control and Prevention reports that drug overdose deaths numbered 8,048 in 1999. And fewer than 20 years later, in 2017, more than 70,200 Americans died from drug overdoses. In that number, depressants, opioids, and antidepressants are responsible for more overdose deaths (45%) than cocaine, heroin, methamphetamine, and amphetamines (39%) combined.

More people report using controlled prescription drugs than cocaine, heroin, and methamphetamine combined. This is no surprise considering that the U.S. makes up 5 percent of the world's population and consumes approximately 80 percent of the world's opioid drugs. The 80 percent figure for U.S. consumption has been cited in various studies, including a 2014 December Express Scripts report. In the U.S. alone, an estimated 54 million people over the age of 12 have used prescription drugs for non-medical reasons in their lifetime. The National Safety Council released survey results showing that 99 percent of doctors are prescribing highly addictive opioid medicines for longer than the three-day period recommended by the Centers for Disease Control and Prevention (CDC). Twenty-three percent of those doctors said they prescribe at least a month's worth of opioids even though the evidence shows that 30-day use causes brain changes that can lead to addiction. The survey also revealed that 71 percent of doctors prescribe opioids for chronic back pain, and 55 percent prescribe them for dental pain—neither of which is appropriate in most cases. The vast majority of doctors continue prescribing these drugs, regardless of the finding that fifty percent of patients were more likely to visit their doctor again if he or she offered alternatives to opioids. Does a doctor's financial gain over the patients' best interests play a role in this behavior?

According to the CDC, alcohol poisoning kills six people in the U.S. every day (88,000 every year), with more than 15 million people struggling with an alcohol addiction. Those that don't consider themselves alcoholics still turn to it periodically. More than 65 million Americans reported binge drinking in March and April of 2018, which was more than 40 percent of the total of then current alcohol users. The numbers have since grown. Results from the National Epidemiologic Survey on Alcohol and Related Conditions in *JAMA Psychiatry* show that the number of Americans who are regularly drinking alcohol has grown substantially over the past decade and surpassed historical numbers and a growing number of them are drinking to a point that's dangerous or harmful.

Food is another substance we use to fill the 'void'. Overeating is linked to a way some people deal with negative emotions. According to the most recent National Health and Nutrition Examination Survey, 18.5 percent of children and nearly 40 percent of adults had obesity in 2015–2016. These are the highest rates ever documented by NHANES. In 1980, the national obesity rate was 12.7 percent.

Something is happening and it's not resulting in healthy lives. Could our food quality and the marketing and promotion of certain unhealthful foods be a contributing factor?

We have created a culture that says you should not have to tolerate any pain. We have taken this concept to greater heights in that we have developed an intolerance for any kind of discomfort and even the slightest pain and are trying to escape from it. Many of these addictions lead to other illnesses that in turn require additional medication, which leave us feeling like victims. Could this relate to an abdication of personal power?

I believe that the habitual taking of any type of substance to relieve whatever type of pain you have isn't moving you away from that pain, it's keeping you focused on it.

I would like you to consider that growth is uncomfortable and sometimes painful. If we are constantly trying to avoid any pain (feeling less than perfect or happy), we are avoiding our own growth. Life is not pain free. Giving birth to a child is painful versus pain free, yet is a positive, life-affirming experience and one that I've heard most women say they wouldn't trade for anything.

In the book *The Coddling of the American Mind*, authors Greg Lukianoff and Jonathan Haidt effectively point out, "A culture that allows the concept of 'safety' to creep so far that it equates emotional discomfort with physical danger is a culture that encourages people to systematically protect one another from the very experiences embedded in daily life that they need in order to become strong and healthy." They describe *safetyism* as a belief system where safety trumps everything else, no matter how unlikely or trivial the potential danger. *Safetyism* demands that your emotions be protected from those that disagree with you as much as your physical being be protected from car accidents. But, rather than strengthening us, this concept makes us more fragile, less resilient, and ultimately weaker. We are experiencing this phenomenon today, particularly with the current college-age generation (iGen).

Coddling and enabling each other to stay in the state of mind of victimization does not promote health, real connection, growth, excellence, or joy. I will discuss accountability in an upcoming chapter and I invite you to hold yourself and those you love accountable for who they are being.

How Angry Are You?

Do you find yourself being angry? If so, what about? The Southern Poverty Law Center's report has found that the number of hate groups across the United States increased for the fourth year in a row in 2018. There are now 1,020 in total, a 7 percent increase on 2018 and a 30 percent jump on 2014. Back in 1999, there were only 457. FBI statistics show that hate crimes increased by 30 percent in the three-year period ending in 2017. That only counts those that were reported and documented.

FBI and leading criminologists define a mass shooting as a single attack in a public place in which four or more victims are killed. Researchers at Harvard University corroborated a study from the FBI that determined that mass shootings have tripled in frequency in recent years. The year 2017 was the worst year on record for mass shootings numbering 346 with 437 deaths and 1,803 people wounded. The following year, 2018, didn't fare much better with 340 shootings. Much anger and hate is festering. The number of websites that attack and malign an entire class of people is astounding and the number of followers is even more so. Consider the battle over gay rights or the right for a woman to choose. Why is what another person does in the bedroom or to their own body such a huge and righteous concern to so many? What if a choice regarding some part of your body was taken away from you? If you believe in religious freedom—which is a right under the Constitution—do you want someone imposing their religion on you if your religious views are different? Thus the word choice. Why are racial tensions increasing in certain areas rather than decreasing? And why do so many people want to spend their time tearing down others instead of creating and uplifting themselves?

If you feel someone is doing something that goes against your belief system, or that you regard as morally wrong, consider that you may not have an understanding of where they are coming from, or what may be right for them under circumstances you may not be able to imagine. Find that thing that you can focus on that is greater than your hate, such as your love for peace in your neighborhood or your love of making sure your children are safe and cared for. The side you hate is probably hurting just as much as the side you are on and an attempt at peace and understanding can go a long way. Destruction doesn't achieve goals, it only creates more problems. Hate is not a solution.

With hate comes anger; both result from fear. Fear of what? Most often it's something like being afraid of being or seeming weak, being ostracized from a particular group or from your friends, feeling threatened about something such as your beliefs—

what if they aren't what you thought them to be, then you would have to change them (the feeling that you've lived your life based on a lie is very threatening). Often the root of our fears can be found in our stories.

Brené Brown, a noted researcher studying vulnerability, courage, worthiness, and shame, studied shame for years and discovered that when we feel shame we lash out, not so much because of what we're lashing out at, rather because of the shame, inadequacy, vulnerability, and insecurity we feel about ourselves. Men are particularly prone to this kind of anger because they don't have as much of a socially built-in outlet, at least not one they immediately perceive to be there, as much as women, to talk through their fears and vulnerabilities; therefore, men either get pissed off or shut down. Women can also react with layers of anger but in a different way, often with layers of emotional outbursts and passive-aggressive behavior. For all of us, this behavior changes with self-awareness and none of us has to be at the whims of our immediate triggers. These are simplifications and generalizations on the subject; therefore, for an in-depth look at how shame and vulnerability affects you, you may want to read Brown's book *Daring Greatly*. Her studies reveal our reactive selves. The self that is at the mercy of our emotions. What is essential to recognize is that we can choose to be consciously aware and cognizant of the fact that we have a choice in whether or not to allow our emotions to rule us. We can choose to engage our personal power.

If you find yourself hating or being angry with someone or something, consider what it means and what it says about you. For example: let's say you're angry about all the work/overwork and redo's you're having to do at your job. You're also angry at people making mistakes and you not catching them and at your boss for ridiculously tight deadlines. What's the real fear? That the result won't succeed and you will come across as incompetent? That someone else will do a better job? That another will reap the rewards before you can finish and that you are less worthy? That the financial gain won't be there and you are on your way to failing? That you keep doing for them what they need to be doing or learning for themselves, but you won't ask for what you want and need? Or, are you angry because it's making you realize that you don't really like what you do?

Sometimes anger at something or someone is a projection of anger at ourselves that we cannot consciously see. Is it that you see someone else boldly living their truth and it shines a light on the fact that you don't have the courage to do that and now you feel it may be too late or that you don't measure up? Is it that you didn't do something thoroughly enough and now things are popping up that you wouldn't have had to spend your time on if you'd done it correctly in the first place? Is it that you made a poor choice and now have to live with it, but don't like it and don't know how to change it so you take it out on others? Is it that you set something in motion and now there's no way to stop it and you fear disaster ahead? Is your ego strongly attached to being right that despite overwhelming new evidence or growth (evolution) on your part, you can't let go of an old conviction? Do you feel the need to push on despite what it's doing to you because you don't want to seem weak?

Anger is stressful. The next time you feel angry ask yourself, "What am I afraid of?" Fear is a perceived possible outcome based on anxiety and worst-case scenarios. It is something you project. It

50

is not reality. Aside from a life-threatening situation where fear is helpful, the fear I am referring to is more often than not self-imposed. The basis or root for most of the fears that create obstacles for you can be found in your story. Examine your story for the elements of fear, look for its roots, and find another perspective before you let fear stand in your way of being the person you can and want to be.

Everyone has a story. Everyone allows their story to determine their choices. Examining yours could prove to be an incredibly valuable tool allowing you to forge new directions in your life. Scars or wounds only show us where we've been. They don't dictate where we're going. Change your perspective on your story—change your life.

Author Anne Morrow Lindberg wrote that "Only in growth, reform and change, paradoxically enough, is true security to be found."

Reflections:

1. What is something that you wish to stop attracting into your life (a type of person, event, circumstance) but that keeps showing up over and over again? What are some beliefs a person might have that would result in that type of pattern?

2. Think of an incident in your life where you didn't stand up for what you knew was right or simply ignored what was happening? Why?

3. Where do you feel victimized? What kind of person wouldn't be a victim in that situation?

4. What repeatedly makes you angry? Why? What can you do about it?

Chapter Four

LIVING AS YOU BELIEVE

Living as you believe requires thought and intention. There are many examples of public figures who do not live as they believe. They tell us that we shouldn't do something, then we find out that they are doing that very thing. For example: the radio talk-show host whose platform was vehemently against drugs, then it came to light that he is a major addict and wound up in rehab; the politician who runs on a platform of family values, then is discovered to have had a series of affairs and fathered children he refuses to claim; and the leader who claims he will protect the most vulnerable of his citizens, then does the exact opposite. These are examples of individuals who are not in alignment with what they say they believe or are not whom they say they are. Do you excuse such behavior in public figures you support? If you do, you need to ask yourself why you believe that it is okay to preach one thing and malign people who don't adhere to that thing and then not adhere to it yourself. Does that kind of behavior make sense? What if you expected and asked of your leaders to be people who set an example of what a great human being is like and one that inspires us all to be better?

When you say one thing but do another you block your ability to create. Your words are important and, at the same time, actions surpass words. In any type of relationship—parent/child, teacher/student, boss/ employee, lovers, friends—you lose credibility every time you behave differently from what you say you believe or what you are asking of someone else. Loss of credibility translates into loss of trust as well. You also lose power in your manifesting ability because you are sending mixed messages to the universe. The result is chaos.

Too often people are afraid to speak up and to stand up for what they really believe. A great visual example of how this happens is in the film 42, the story of Jackie Robinson, the first African American major league baseball player. At that time in 1946 America, it was culturally expected that if you were white you didn't associate with other races. To have a star player not be a white man was uncomfortable and the masses reacted to their discomfort by rejecting and booing Jackie. In the film, a young, caucasian boy is in the stands with his father and is enthralled and excited by Jackie and his incredible talent. He is coming from a genuine place of having no preconceived notions or biases against the man's color.

He is seeing what is real and is about to cheer for Jackie when he witnesses his father and other men booing and hurling names at the athlete for being Black. In that moment, instead of following his truth, the boy mimics his father and suppresses his real instincts.

The example above doesn't apply just to children. Some people go with the flow or their peer group so they don't get shunned, or they stand by a party line or popular statement without thinking because it makes them appear cool in the moment or be a part of something. Or they go along with a belief or idea because one of their friends or a celebrity or someone they think is powerful is saying they should. Many politicians today make statements that they don't believe, when the facts don't support their statements. When they attempt to twist the facts to either inject fear or to foster support for a policy they are pushing or to say what they need to say to get elected. As an example, refugees from Central America were making their way through Mexico heading for the United States attempting to seek asylum from persecution, poverty, and violence. Before they even reached Mexico City, President Trump labeled them as an immediate looming threat, an invasion filled with gang members and very bad people who would storm our border. The President deployed an unprecedented amount of military resources to the border and induced fear to attempt to gain support for building a wall and more stringent immigration policies, including separating children from their parents. Another example is politicians claiming that although they propose repealing the current AMA health care policy they are for ensuring that pre-existing conditions will not be excluded from new coverage, yet that very protection was cut from the bill they were attempting to push through. Some politicians present themselves as something they're not, believing that that's what they have to say or do to get elected. Those ideas come from polls and the press, which may not be accurate. Imagine what the world would be like if the people seeking elected office simply spoke from their real beliefs and from whom they really are instead of trying to fit into categories of sound bites and party lines. Authenticity takes clarity, conviction, courage, and humility that challenges all of us. Remaining authentic in an environment of gotcha games from opponents and sensationalist reporting is extremely difficult, yet possible if we as the citizens and consumers respond to it and demand more of it.

When asked what you believe in, many people say they believe in their faith, such as a spiritual or religious perspective. But that does not reveal the kind of beliefs I am referring to here; it's only a piece. Citing a religious doctrine doesn't reveal what's at your core and what lives in your subconscious. If you say you believe in your faith, whatever faith that is, what you are saying is that you believe in a moral dictate. The question then becomes, how do you believe in that dictate? Absolutely and rigidly? A belief that a higher authority (and not you) governs your morals without exception? A belief that an old doctrine and the enforcers of that doctrine know better than you what is morally right for you in every circumstance? Or are you flexible with broader and more nuanced views? When you look at your faith, are you clear about what you mean by faith and how it shows up in your behavior?

Your mind is the most powerful tool you have. Where your thoughts go, reality follows. Training and managing your mind is the most important skill you can have. Our existence happens in four different realms—the physical world, the mental world, the emotional world, and the spiritual world. We manifest our way through life first through our thoughts, which lead to feelings, which then lead to actions that lead to results.

As adults, our beliefs initially come from past programming. Your past programming happened in childhood as you grew into the world in three primary ways. Your verbal programming developed as a result of what you heard when you were young.

Your modeled behavior came as a result of what you saw. And last, specific incidents that you experienced created beliefs that rooted in your subconscious. Those beliefs were created by what you chose to perceive and made up about what you heard, saw, and experienced. We are exposed to many things that are good for us and often we don't choose to focus on those. We choose our programming. Most people have past programming that in some area of life isn't helping them, and actually prevents them in achieving the kind of life they want.

The first step in creating a chosen future for yourself is to examine your programming and become aware of some of the things you heard growing up that don't serve you. Some examples are: "People like you aren't talented enough to _____"; "Our people arc always taken advantage of"; "Life is a constant struggle"; "Life is hard"; "Money is the root of all evil"; and so on.

Second, notice how your parents, family members, role models, and guardians behaved as you were growing up and what messages they modeled to you. Were they always struggling? Did they have big successes followed by big losses? Were they bitter? Did they pretend everything was always wonderful when it wasn't? The myriad of messages is endless. We make interpretations from all of these experiences and create our own story from them.

Lastly, take a look at specific incidents that had an impact on you. Ask yourself if there are any events that somehow became linked to pain, struggle, hardship, lack of self-esteem, shame, or loss. Once you become aware of some of these things, the next step is to understand from where your way of thinking originates and that it came from outside of you. Once you realize that your past way of thinking isn't who you are or who you want to be, you can separate yourself from it and choose to keep it or let it go depending on whether is serves your goals or not.

Author Robert Allen said, "No thought lives in your head rent-free." You will pay in money, energy, time, health, and level of happiness for your negative thoughts. Examine your thoughts carefully, then determine whether they are empowering or disempowering. Do you hear a stream of excuses in your head of why you can't do or be something great, or voices of doubt at every turn, or examples of what could and likely will go wrong? Do you hear reasons for why your happiness or success is impossible? These are disempowering thoughts that prevent you from the next steps necessary for your happiness, health, and success.

We all have core beliefs that are the architects of our lives. In looking at your story, you will come across some of your beliefs. You will be tempted to dismiss, deny, or excuse some of the beliefs you see. Those are the most valuable ones to explore. For example, if you are always broke, what beliefs about money do you hold? Or is it about your self-worth? There's a disempowering belief in there somewhere. If you have a circumstance in your life (not being able to keep a partner, regularly losing jobs, friends who betray you, etc.) that points to a belief that you consciously would deny, I invite you to look again. There may be a transparent belief in there. A belief that draws circumstances and people into your life that you claim not to want, yet they seem to pop up over and over again.

If deep down you believe you can't, then you can't and won't be able to. If you believe you will be thwarted, then you will. You can't intend to do or achieve a thing if you don't believe it is possible.

We each have a powerful driving force inside of ourselves that can make any vision or dream a reality, as long as our beliefs support it.

The fabric of your personal world comes down to your beliefs. Not your neighbor's beliefs, not social beliefs, but yours alone, as to whether something is attainable for you, including how you want to show up in the world and be seen. In the realm of possibility, there is no division between beliefs and action, mind and body, dream and reality. If you say you desire a thing and haven't been able to fulfill that desire and it feels as if it's impossible to ever have it, ask yourself what has stood in your way? Now take that list, item by item, and see what obstacles exist. For example, I didn't have the money, or I'm not tall enough, or I can't get a break. Can you do something to overcome the obstacle? If your answer is no, why not? Some obstacles are unchangeable —your age and the laws of physics, for example. But most can be worked with. What belief do you hold about what you are not getting that makes it impossible? As long as you believe a thing, the world around you will reflect that belief back to you. This is because your beliefs are creating your world and the human ego vehemently defends and wants to prove true those beliefs. Why? Because most people desire to be right more than they desire the thing they claim they want if it would unravel the deep fabric of their beliefs. Silly? On a logical level, yes. But on an emotional level the roots go deep. When our subconscious mind must choose between beliefs deeply rooted in emotion or the arena of logic, most of the time our emotions win.

A great danger is to simply latch on to a belief because someone else told you that it's the right one. To believe a thing in order to fit in to a particular group can prove to be disempowering to your health in the long run.

Let's bring back the discussion of focus and how it relates to your beliefs. You cannot discover new oceans until you have the courage to lose sight of the shore. If a belief you hold isn't serving you well, let it go and shift your focus to a more affirming belief.

Too often people focus on what is not working for them. In so doing they don't realize that they continue to attract the things that don't work because they are reinforcing their focus of "it's not working." Author and motivational speaker T. Harv Eker said, "When you are complaining, you become a living, breathing 'crap magnet.'" This is not to say that one shouldn't take into account what wasn't effective so as not to repeat it and to make adjustments. That is different than remaining focused on the failings and reinforcing the beliefs that go with them.

Let's take a person who is miserable because they claim they can't live how they wish off of the money they earn. They remain focused on what they can't buy, or do, and everywhere they look they see what they can't have. That person must release their focus on their not having it in order to begin attracting some "haves" into their life. They must also release the belief that this is the way life is for them and they're stuck. The releasing of that focus is difficult because it's familiar, it's comfortable, it's what they know, and it's scary to think they might have been able to control making a change all along.

When you hit a snag in your plans, does your mind immediately go to the worst-case scenario, "OMG this is not going to happen," or "Of course nothing can run smoothly," or to a recital of Murphy's law "anything that can go wrong will go wrong"? The surge of anxiety created by such negative thinking creates tremendous stress and energetic blocks for you to have to overcome, even though they may be unseen. When faced with a hurdle, do you really want to create more stuff to get over?

Worrying is familiar and a way to avoid problem solving. I have friends whose parents were extreme worriers and that modeled behavior, from their childhood, was passed on to them. A small dose of worry can actually catapult you into action and that can improve your performance when working on a cognitively demanding task, such as a test or exam. Moderate levels of worry can improve functioning and performance. But when worry is heightened, there is a decline in performance. Examine the beliefs that underlie your worries. When you allow worry to turn to the negative, remember— where your focus goes, your reality follows. Once you are aware of your level of worry it's easier to handle and to put it toward good use. When you know it's there you realize that your next step is to prepare for taking action toward what is worrying you. That realization will immediately begin to turn your focus to your options instead of your obsession with the negative.

In an interview, John Lennon revealed, "When I was five years old, my mother always told me that happiness was the key to life. When I went to school, they asked me what I wanted to be when I grew up. I wrote down 'happy.' They told me I didn't understand the assignment, and I told them they didn't understand life."

What you focus on grows and expands. What are you focused on? Opportunities or obstacles? This can inform you of your beliefs. Think about it and choose deliberately.

Think for Yourself

American poet and philosopher Henry David Thoreau said, "I know of no more encouraging fact than the unquestionable ability of man to elevate himself by conscious endeavor." Our ability to be self-aware is what separates us from animals and what gives us the ability to advance. To lose sight of your experiences and buy into another's thoughts about a matter without your own analysis and investigation can be a dangerous thing. Information is valuable. However, partial information can be quite precarious and lead you astray. As long as you are willing to trust your instincts and to look at all the information available and at all sides and to not simply follow another's propaganda, your own assessments will serve you well. First and foremost, consider the source of the particular information. What is the writer/speaker's motivation? Do they have an agenda or a cause to further? Second, consider your own experiences and encounters and see if anything aligns to what they are saying, then go further into other types of research and verification if necessary. If someone tells you to not read something or to not look at a body of information either on the Internet or books or statistics or facts or science, then the first question you should ask is why?

We are living in a world filled with an inordinate amount of overstimulation in the form of social media targeting, news and information (both fake and real), and media designed to incite rather than inform. These things tug at our emotions from a base and unbounded place all for the sake of a sale or a power play. Some of us react because we don't give ourselves time to think. The thing we are reacting to triggers us in some way and we jump on it, instead of taking a breath and thinking it through. Others don't take the time to think because it's easier to react. Still others merely go about their days performing robotic functions because it's unchallenging. Most of us can find an example of our being guilty of one or more of these kinds of reactions. Those reactions sap us of our power, both individually and collectively. I ask you to consider changing that paradigm.

Reactive people tend to be followers. The reason for this is because it's easier. To follow is to push off responsibility onto others, whether it be your parents, your community's pressure, a political dictate, social and religious rules and barriers, your boss, your economic circumstances, or your choice of daily celebrity. We are getting closer to becoming a world where self responsibility is nearing extinction. I witnessed a recent encounter between a customer and cashier at a deli that exemplifies what I'm talking about: The special of the day was a slice of pizza, a soda, and a salad for $8.95. The customer asked for the special. When the cashier handed him a glass, the customer declined it, saying he didn't want the soda. The cashier then rang him up for $10.95 plus tax. The customer pointed out that the special was listed for the lesser price. The cashier responded, "I can't give you the special because you don't want the drink." The customer attempted explaining that he was ordering the special and saving them by not taking the drink—that he was actually saving the establishment time and money—but the cashier remained firm. This kind of complete lack of thought occurs every day and slowly, one incident at a time, and adds to the mountain of frustrations, obstacles, and problems that can be avoided if only we encouraged and insisted upon thoughtful presence in our daily lives.

Reactivity happens instantly from an emotional trigger combined with lack of thought. Reactive people are at the mercy of what comes at them. In contrast, proactivity requires conscious and deliberate thought and consideration. Proactive behavior is a function of our decisions, not our conditions, and requires taking responsibility for our actions, which includes a willingness to accept the consequences that will result.

Renown psychiatrist Viktor Frankl recognized that the most basic habit in successful and highly effective people is proactivity. This doesn't simply mean that successful people are those who do things. Proactivity means that you recognize that you are responsible for your life and that your behavior is a function of your decisions, not your conditions.

To be proactive is to have the initiative and responsibility to make things happen in your life. Highly successful people recognize their responsibility and they do not blame circumstances, conditions, or their upbringing for their behavior. In the book *The 7 Habits of Highly Effective People*, author Stephen Covey said, "[Proactive] behavior is a product of their conscious choices, based on values, rather than a product of their conditions, based on feeling...Reactive people are often affected by their physical and emotional environment...Proactive people can carry their own weather with them."

Which would you rather be? Reactive or proactive? Your choice begins with thought. Your thoughts (along with your beliefs) lead to your actions, which leads to your results. The power of your mind and your ability to act takes you where you want to go. Ask yourself—are you present and consciously aware of what you're doing when you do it? Do you think through the tasks of your life? Do you blame others for your life not being how you wish it to be or do you take steps to make necessary changes?

Former First Lady Eleanor Roosevelt said, "No one can hurt you without your consent." Many of us often consent to what happens to us (even if by just staying), rather than protest. I invite you to take a moment and think before you speak or act. Think about where you want to be, who you want to be, what results your words or actions may have, then go forth and be proactive.

Always look and consider the source of whatever you are contemplating or considering. The power of thought is our gift as humans and that incorporates your instincts as well—your basic gut evaluations. A mother instinctively senses when her child is vulnerable or in danger and knows it's wrong to abandon a child in need, no matter what anyone else says.

A great way to build your confidence in your own thoughts is to educate yourself and to keep educating yourself. As discussed before, there are many ways of learning: personal experiences, reading, all types of media, classes, mentors, observation, and more. If the idea of continuously learning and growing turns you off, consider a few things:

* If you aren't learning about new things you aren't experiencing new things.

* Being stagnant doesn't last long. You either grow or you die. An applicable saying is "if you don't use it you lose it," and a basic example is our muscles, if you don't use a muscle it atrophies. The same is true of your brain.

* In pursuing knowledge, you encounter a wider array of

people and can deepen and even discover new interests and new kindsof relationships.

* With wisdom comes choice. Greater knowledge brings more options and life choices you wouldn't otherwise know or consider. Wisdom and knowledge bring you ideas about how to solve problems you may have thought you had to live with, how to get out of a particular situation you thought hopeless, and how to achieve or do something you thought you could only dream about.

Earl Nightingale, an early American radio personality and author, said that a person who thinks about nothing becomes nothing. I would like to offer an excerpt from his book *The Strangest Secret*. If it sparks some interest, you may want to consider reading his work. Here it is:

> *"How does it work? Why do we become what we think about? Well, I'll tell you how it works, as far as we know. To do this, I want to tell you about a situation that parallels the human mind.*
>
> *"Suppose a farmer has some land, and it's good, fertile land. The land gives the farmer a choice; he may plant in that land whatever he chooses. The land doesn't care. It's up to the farmer to make the decision. We're comparing the human mind with the land because the mind, like the land, doesn't care what you plant in it. It will return what you plant, but it doesn't care what you plant.*

"Now, let's say that the farmer has two seeds in his hand—one is a seed of corn, the other is nightshade, a deadly poison. He digs two little holes in the earth and he plants both seeds—one corn, the other nightshade, He covers up the holes, waters and takes care of the land…and what will happen? Invariably, the land will return what was planted…."

So, what happened? Two plants grew. One was edible, the other was poisonous.

As Nightingale stated, the mind, like soil, doesn't care what you plant in it. However, the mind is much more fertile, more complex, mysterious, and nuanced than soil, and I believe more powerful, but it works in much the same way. If the thoughts and beliefs you plant are around a specific, worthwhile goal, you will reach that goal. Sometimes it may not look like you thought it would, but the seed will grow, because what we plant will return certain results to us.

Think about who you are right now. If you succumb to seeing yourself as a victim, you will continue reinforcing that in your life. You have the power to create your life according to your vision and the first step is in believing that and being accountable for your thoughts.

Thomas Edison said, "There are few people who think, a few more who think they think, and then there are the great majority, who would rather die than think."

Rather than just following along or being in that majority, consider thinking for yourself. Our greatest gift as a species is the ability to think and the power of our thoughts. Take back your power, be proactive, and think for yourself.

Reflections:

1. When was there a time or a belief you adopted that you later realized what you believed wasn't truth or fact? Did you still go along with the old belief or did you evolve with the new information?

2. Do you follow the rules in situations where you want to ascend, such as in your job or a social group, if those rules don't make sense, may not be ethical, or could potentially hurt someone, or do you question them?

3. Think of a social or professional situation where someone said something slanderous or lied or held up as fact that which wasn't. Did you speak up or remain silent? Why?

4. Are you religious? Why or why not? How did you choose your religion? What about it do you like? What don't you like?

Chapter Five
DIG DEEPER

All of us have a unique outlook on the world and on whom we believe we are. As with other things in life, when we are too close to a situation, we may not have the full perspective.

Another great exercise for a viewpoint on yourself is to take a look at the people in your life. Like attracts like and energy is contagious. If you are an exceptionally talented pianist and are surrounded by master pianists or people who support you in your piano playing and excelling, then chances are you will achieve something with your talent. If, however, you are surrounded by people who don't appreciate your talent, degrade it, tell you that piano playing is a hobby, that no one really makes a living at it and you're not that good and do whatever they can to keep you from doing it, then unless you find a way to break free from those attitudes you will have a very difficult time achieving greatness as a pianist.

Did you know that most people earn within twenty percent of the average income of their closest friends? If your friends and family are all broke and have nothing but negative things to say about anyone with money and you would like to earn much more, then perhaps the clue lies here. Subconsciously you may believe that you will no longer be liked by your family and friends if you become wealthy because you want to be liked by them.

If you want to excel in a talent, a hobby, a study, or in your income, then choose the people you spend a lot of time with very carefully. Seek out those whom you admire, those with whom you share a point of view, and those with whom you feel energized and positive.

Regardless of how you got there, you are accountable for wherever you currently are in your life and you have the power to choose how and who to be in your situation, even if your situation is dire. If you are in a difficult situation, blaming others won't solve the problem.

Look at your interests and the people you applaud and how you support them. Who they are, combined with your own behavior toward others, says a great deal about how you feel about yourself, your level of belief in yourself, and can give you some insight into who you are.

Real estate tycoon Nathan Shapell claimed that once you see how a person does business, how they behave when they drink, and how they play golf, you will know all the key things you need to know about that person. The reason that many people can gauge another's overall character from one or two areas in life is because our minds have a habit of carrying out the same beliefs and behavioral patterns across the spectrum in our lives. If you know someone who is always late to anything you ever invite them to, chances are you are not the only one having that experience with that person. Some people become known for being chronically late.

Many of us know someone who says, "Oh this old thing" or "I didn't do anything, I was just here" or "Don't be silly, I'm not..." and any variation thereof instead of simply saying "thank you" to a compliment. If you are a person who regularly deflects compliments, perhaps that is evidence that you are not good at receiving marvelous things in your life. Brushing off a compliment may seem like a negligible thing, even a humble thing, but chances are that a simple thing like that is also an indicator of how other things happen, or don't happen, in your life.

If you are suspicious of people who give you compliments or gifts or opportunities that seem really good, then consider that your suspicion will deflect those whose motives are pure and attract those who will give you reason to be suspicious because in the overall scheme of your life the universe delivers to you what you believe and what you expect to receive.

Secretary of State under Eisenhower John Foster Dulles said that "A man's accomplishments in life are the cumulative effect of his attention to detail." I, too, believe that little things matter a lot, because one by one they create the picture of who you are. One of my favorite T. Harv Eker sayings is "How you do anything is how you do everything."

If you are conscientious about keeping your home clean, then chances are your office will also be clean. If you say you want to plant a garden and buy all the things you need but never complete it, or say you will paint a room and only paint one or half of a wall, or say you will clean out a closet and only stuff more junk in there, then chances are that you also have a hard time following through on other things. There are thousands of examples of not following through or not completing things and that becomes a pattern. That pattern may be less visible in some areas of your life where its repercussions are more transparent but it's still there and may require deeper examination. For example, you want to advance in your job, and know that you must spend a weekend at a task, but for every weekend that comes up, you put it off until the opportunity vanishes. Or you tell a friend that you will read something they've written or look at a business plan, but every time they mention it, you make the promise again for next time you get together until it becomes irrelevant and ultimately the friend gives up believing that you will ever do it. Perhaps later you learn that what the friend didn't tell you is that they were considering hiring you in some capacity, but realized that you couldn't be counted on.

Fielding Adversity

Most people believe that we, as humans, can reach higher and achieve more and continue to progress and innovate beyond where we are now and what we think we know now. But, very few actually take this to heart and apply it in their own lives. When it comes to our own lives, the excuses pile up as to why we are not achieving our heights. What you believe creates your reality. Not what you theoretically and consciously believe in general, but what you actually believe about yourself.

Are you someone who believes you can achieve more greatness but only under certain circumstances that come together easily and without opposition? Or are you someone who believes others can achieve far more than you because of their luck or specific circumstances? We all have to assess where we are before we can move forward. It is true that some people have a shorter distance to travel than others and some have fewer obstacles than others. This is how we are tested. Adversity strikes in different ways for different people. Your obstacles may seem far more insurmountable than that other person's, but we never truly know another's inner demons and making assumptions will get you nowhere. Your focus should remain on yourself. Some people are only willing to do what it takes to a certain point and go no further; if they don't get certain results, they quit. They stop because it becomes comfortable in that place and they don't feel the need for more or are too afraid to go any further. Other people are willing to do what it takes to achieve their goals. They are compelled and willing to do what it takes to keep striving and breaking barriers and limits throughout their lives regardless of how long it takes and the setbacks they encounter along the way.

There is no right or wrong way to be; understanding which type of person you are can help you achieve a certain level of peace and contentment so that either you can change that which you want to change or you can accept yourself and not feel compelled to apologize for not wanting more or feel guilty for not having achieved what you thought you "should". This understanding needs to incorporate your real desires and the specifics for why you desire them. For example, if you are the type of person who only goes so far then quits, you must first understand why you quit. If your "why" is not a destructive mechanism or a fear to be overcome, but instead it is something more important to you than the achievement itself, then you can make peace with it.

A good way for you to explore your underlying beliefs about what is possible for you is to examine how you act during times of adversity. Those times include periods of financial scarcity, getting married, death of a loved one, infidelity (either you or the other person), serious illness, divorce or other breakup, loss of something treasured, and other crises that feel overwhelming.

When faced with adversity do you...

A. Withdraw, fall apart. and find yourself unable to deal with your circumstances?

B. Become hardened, stiffen and put up walls, and become suspicious?

C. Learn from the experience, grow, and evolve as a result?

Most people would like to think of themselves as being the type of person who chooses C in adversity and, yet, you must first begin by being honest. If you are not there yet, then begin your journey. Grow yourself bigger so that you can deal with the circumstances you are dealt and practice a flexible mind and heart so that you don't find yourself facing a strong wind that inevitably breaks you, but rather one that you can bend through.

Your Perspective

How do you look at the world? Glass half empty or half full? Your perspective has everything to do with whom you are being in any given moment. For most people, as we get older, we create a more and more structured framework for ourselves and for our lives, limiting our ability to see different possibilities. This type of restrictive structure, that we settle into over time, also limits our ability to see other people's viewpoints.

The majority of blocks people experience in their lives tend to stem from a framework of assumptions they carry with them from their early years as well as those created throughout their life experiences. If you don't believe the world allows certain things to happen, you can be sure that your world will reinforce that belief and those things will not appear possible in your world view. Many people have heard the story how the Native Americans didn't "see" the large ships as they came toward the Eastern shore. We don't know how they perceived the ships or what they actually did or did not see, but it's safe to assert that they may not have identified the ships as such since they had no visual concept of such a thing in their framework.

In the book *The Art of Possibility* Rosamund Stone Zander and Benjamin Zander write, "We perceive only the sensations we are programmed to receive, and our awareness is further restricted by the fact that we recognize only those for which we have mental maps or categories." The British neuropsychologist Richard Gregory wrote, "The senses do not give us a picture of the world directly; rather they provide evidence for the checking of hypotheses about what lies before us."

In other words, we could argue that every perception is invented. We each experience a different reality even under the same physical actuality or circumstance. For example, two sisters are walking along the beach. It's a sunny, warm day. Other people are passing them, saying hello and smiling. Some are walking their dogs, others are power walking, still others are jogging or strolling leisurely. One sister notices and comments on the beautiful color of the water, the friendly people, the way the sand feels good on her feet, the interesting architecture of some of the homes along the shore, and the colors of the flowers planted on balconies. This sister smiles at the passersby and greets them and is feeling good. The other sister notices how some of the people around them are power walking, or walking with weights, or jogging, and how gritty the sand feels on her feet. She notices how fit many of these people are and begins to get angry at the narcissistic body-obsessed culture she is seeing. She observes the same homes and comments how those people are shallow and pretentious, that they are money and image obsessed, and how they don't care about "real" people. When they return home, the first sister has enjoyed the beach walk and tunes out the negative comments of the second sister, while the second sister comes home feeling as if she's just witnessed the downfall of humanity. Same physical reality, yet two very different frameworks.

Below is a puzzle of sorts. If you've never seen this before, try to join all nine dots with four straight lines, without taking pen from paper.

If you find it difficult, you are not alone. Most people find themselves instantly classifying the nine dots as a two-dimensional square and that eliminates other possibilities for them and they are stuck. This is a wonderful illustration of how we confine what we perceive to be possible. Every circumstance, problem, issue, or dead-end you encounter in your life only appears unsolvable within a particular point of view. If you break out of your box and create another frame around the information, new paths appear.

By drawing a different construct of assumptions around the same circumstances, you will create for yourself a new view and new pathways where extraordinary accomplishment becomes possible.

The Zanders offer a practice for making this shift. First, ask yourself this question: What assumptions am I making that I'm not aware I'm making that gives me what I see?

Once you've answered that question, then ask yourself: What might I now invent that I haven't yet invented that would give me other choices?

Here is the solution to the puzzle:

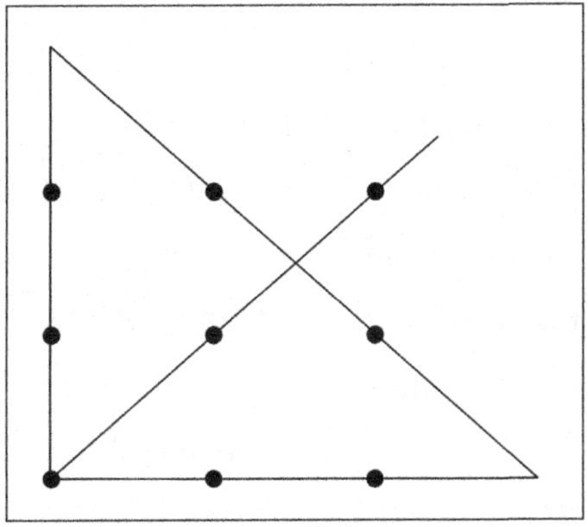

If we invent our worlds, why not invent a foundation for yourself that enhances your life and those around you.

How you see something is how it ultimately becomes. You choose the way you see a thing. And remember, it has no meaning except the one you give it.

Do you believe in magic? One of the definitions of magic is 'a quality that makes something seem removed from everyday life, especially in a way that gives delight.' Aren't we always searching for moments of delight in our lives? Perhaps some of us are simply more astute to pulling the magic out of a situation. Your limits are what you see them to be. Recognize them as illusion and they will cease to be limits.

Author Robert Fulghum tells a wonderful story in his book *All I Really Need To Know I Learned In Kindergarten* about the game Giants, Wizards, and Dwarfs that he played with children seven to ten years old. The purpose of the game involved some intellectual decision-making, but it really was about making a lot of noise, running around chasing people until nobody knew which side they were on or who won. As the kids were running around he yelled, "You have to decide now which you are—a Giant, a Wizard, or a Dwarf!" Kids huddled in groups and whispered amongst each other. All except a young girl who came up to him and asked, "Where do the Mermaids stand?" Robert just looked at her stalling, then she added,

"Yes. You see, I am a Mermaid."

"There are no such things as Mermaids," he retorted.

"Oh, yes, I am one!" This girl did not relate to any of the other labels offered her. She knew her category. Mermaid. And was not about to leave the game and claim defeat. She fully intended to participate, wherever Mermaids fit into the scheme of things. Without giving up dignity or identity. She took it for granted that there was a place for Mermaids and that Fulghum's job was to know where.

Her belief was so ardent that he responded, "The Mermaid stands right here by the King of the sea!"

Where do Mermaids stand? All those who are different, who do not fit the norm, and who do not accept the available boxes and pigeonholes, where do they stand?

We are facing an intolerance among each other in our current cultural climate. A great number of us have put up so many barriers to simply being willing to look at those who are different from us, let alone beginning to understand. So where do Mermaids stand? Fulghum says, "Answer that question and you can build a school, a nation, or a world on it."

Be open and receptive to others, for they always bring value—whether in the form of a lesson, a clue, a direction, a connection, a comfort, a joy, or merely a distraction.

Wherever you live, whatever you do, you touch other people's lives in ways that you may not even be aware of. There are people who brush by us in a crowd, whose eyes we may catch on a train that evokes a potent feeling, those who depend on us, watch us, learn from us and take from us.

There is an old story of a good man who was granted one wish by God. The man said he would like to go about doing good without knowing about it. His wish was granted. God then decided that it was such a good idea, he would grant that wish to all human beings...and here we are.

What You Value

Let's suppose that a person says they value excellence. When producing a film, if a studio needs to make a decision between what marketing tells them will make more sales and what is a more intelligent story or stronger, deeper plot line, nearly one hundred percent of the time the studio goes with the bigger sell. For a blockbuster market, studios will dumb down a script to appeal to the lowest common denominator instead of choosing to stretch people's minds and raise the bar on their thinking because it means immediate, larger profits. They don't think long range. Sacrificing a long-term vision for short-term gains is becoming a disease spreading in all areas of business all over the world. But because the film they chose to release made a lot of money, some would argue that they have excelled at their job because they have achieved profits. If money is their measure of excellence, then that is true. However, under this test, excellence isn't the underlying value, money is. And an immediate measure of it, rather than a long range one.

Whom you work for and/or how you run your business has a huge impact not only as a reflection of who you are, but also on society as a whole. Unfortunately, large corporations have often become blind to the effects they have on the environment and on people on a grander scale. But large corporations are made up of individuals, so the problem must lie in the individuals (the leaders) who place profit for profits' sake above all else.

In South America, the deforestation of the Amazon is reaching alarming proportions. As indigenous people have intuitively grasped for centuries, the benefits the Amazon provides are of immeasurable worth. Those benefits include: water cycling (the forest produces not only half its own rainfall but much of the rain south of the Amazon and east of the Andes), carbon sequestering (by holding and absorbing carbon dioxide, the forest mitigates global warming and cleanses the atmosphere), and maintenance of an unmatched diversity of life. Nature has perfected excellence at creating the biosphere. But the marketplace has yet to assign a value to the forest. It's far more profitable, in the short run, to cut it down for grazing and farming than to leave it standing.

Look at what the U.S. coal companies have done to the Appalachian Mountains. They have literally cut off the tops of countless mountains to get at the coal, and in so doing have degraded more than 1,200 miles of streams and at least 800 miles were completely buried by valley fills between 1985 and 2001. Today that figure is much more dire. This means that the streams have been filled with toxins and the majority of life in those streams is gone. An increase in flooding and cancer rates in those communities is also a byproduct.

You may be wondering what any of this has to do with your values and the pursuit of excellence. Some could argue that these companies are superb at mining, but they would be wrong because to achieve excellence would be to mine coal without recklessly destroying the environment and the life (including human) within it and to mine without abusing and mistreating workers. Winning and excellence are not synonymous. One is a monetary measure of outdoing someone else, while the other is a value. You could easily win if you have your opponents killed off and there're no competitors and no fair game. In that case, what do you value?

Even doctors have lost merit in their practices. How often do you go to the doctor and they spend barely a few minutes with you and give you a prognosis, some advice, and often a prescription? Is the accuracy of that visit waning? Gone are the days when the majority of us knew our doctors well and they took the time to really know our habits, our histories, and our family. According to the Statistics Portal, today the majority of new doctors spend an average of fewer than 15 minutes with their patients. Apparently the bulk of their time is devoted to paperwork. Bureaucracy is definitely contributing a death blow to excellence in many areas of business.

And the reason? Money. Money over quality. Money over life. Money over long-term benefits. Money as a value above all else. Are we asking the question if our valuing of money over all else is worth is? If the actions we are taking leave us with a dying planet and an unhappy, disconnected, and neurotic humanity, then what is the money worth if we have nothing of value left to spend it on? The truth is we can make money and plenty of it without having to cheat the planet and each other and in a way that would create much more satisfaction.

I am not saying that the pursuit of money is not a worthy goal. I'm saying that your values lie in how you pursue that goal. You've heard the expression that money corrupts or perhaps heard someone refer to wealthy people as "filthy" rich—adding a negative spin onto wealth. I believe that **money only makes you more of who you really are.** Money alone will not make a person corrupt, just as it won't automatically make one generous. Money is important in the areas in which it works and unimportant in the areas in which it doesn't. How you make your money says something about you. It tells the world what you're good at, what you believe about others, what you believe about yourself, what you believe about the world you live in, your outlook on your opportunities and future, and what you value.

Do you believe that in order for you to gain something, another person must lose? That in order for you to eat well, others must eat less or go hungry? In order for you to have a lot of money others must be poorer? If your answer is yes, then you are like the majority of individuals who have a hard time believing that there is enough for everybody. These beliefs stem from fear. There is enough for everybody unless those who have more destroy the ability for others to have simply what they need.

If you come from a place of win/win, where you want not only yourself to win, but those you are dealing with to win as well, you come from and reinforce the belief that there is plenty for everybody and that success is not achieved at the expense of others. This allows you to both value and to act with integrity and humanity.

The concept of win/win should result in mutual benefits in all human interactions. It means that an agreement you make works for all parties to that agreement. If an agreement is made that is win/lose, then one side will remain bitter or seek to right the wrong, or seek vengeance, or pass down the pain he or she endured to others, creating a negative cycle of problems and obstacles that can continue for years or centuries (in the case of certain nations) rather than a peaceful coexistence. A win doesn't always mean that you get what you want. It can mean that you are left with options and means to support or to create your future different from what you may have considered ideal. You are not left destroyed simply for another's benefit. You also have gained something that was necessary for you when you entered the agreement.

Sometimes a person or one side of a situation refuses to allow even the slightest win for the other side. The win/lose model serves those whose egos need constant boosting and attention. At the root these are insecure people masquerading as powerful authorities in their own right. If you set up people in a competition between each other where the conditions are created such that there is only a winner if the others lose, then you eliminate the possibility of cooperation, teamwork and a view toward interdependence. (This does not apply to sports where the underlying agreement between both parties is for one side to outshine the other based on talent.)

The win/win concept creates a positive outcome and longevity. In a win/lose scenario, one side might win for the moment, but what about in the long run? In *The Seven Habits of Highly Effective People*, Stephen Covey illustrates that "If I am a supplier to your company, for example, and I win on my terms in a particular negotiation, I may get what I want now. But will you come to me again? My short-term Win will really be a long-term Lose if I don't get your repeat business." The same is true if you sell something to someone for more than the item is worth or you misrepresent its condition to get the price you want, you will begin to foster a reputation that will hurt you in the future. What value do you place on your reputation?

Negotiating and working toward Win/Win requires consideration, courage, and some vision and concern for the long run. The younger you are, the more difficult you may find understanding that the next year (and even the one after that) should be a consideration in your decision-making, let alone looking ahead several years. But think of it like a relationship; if you want to continue having a good relationship with a person for years, it matters that you both continue to get something out of it.

Character is the foundation of the Win/Win concept and there are three traits and values that are essential to this foundation: Integrity, Maturity, and an Abundance Mentality.

Integrity means that you are honest and have clearly identified values. You keep meaningful promises and commitments that help you develop self-awareness and an independent will.

Maturity is defined as being able to express your feelings and convictions with courage balanced with consideration for the feelings and convictions of others. It is the balance between consideration and courage.

The Abundance Mentality is the knowledge that in some form there is plenty for everyone. This is the foundation for being able to be happy for others' successes, for having a deep inner sense of personal worth and security. It recognizes the unlimited possibilities for positive interactive growth and development. This is in direct contrast to the scarcity mentality. For long term and lasting success, pursuing a win/win mentality is essential. If you say you value integrity, commitment, loyalty and honesty, then your word is crucial. Sometimes you may say what is easiest in the moment, what you think you should say to impress someone, to keep your job, or to look good. You may also have a tendency to say what you think others want to hear. In this way you may make commitments you don't mean to keep, you may express a belief you don't have, or you may make a statement that proves to be untrue and ultimately lessens yourself in the process.

Every time your words come from one of those reasons and not from the things you claim to value, you show the world that you really don't value those things.

Your Word

We've talked about how your thoughts are the seeds to creating your life. The next layer is your word. What you say is a reflection of who you are. If your words don't match your thoughts, the first link in the chain to creating what you want to create is broken. Then if your words don't match your actions, the next link is broken and success in manifesting or achieving your visions becomes that much more difficult, if not impossible. You yourself are the only thing wholly under your control. What you say and how you react to the world around you are a part of what defines you. Your word is your promise. Recipient of the 2005 Gandhi Nonviolence Award Helice Bridges (known as Sparky) makes a case that who you are matters to the world at large and no one is off the hook. She said, "I am not just here to make a living. I am here to make a life." Her entire effort began as one sentence on a blue ribbon—"Who I Am Makes A Difference." Those words resulted in her teaching kids, educators, parents, neighbors, and businesspeople how to express their appreciation; to value uniqueness, respect, and love; and to empower their dreams. Over 40 million people have been touched by her message, her words, and over the years this has resulted in saving lives, ending violence, and making dreams come true.

If you readily do not live up to your word, your word becomes meaningless and gives others the opportunity to dismiss you, to not take you seriously, and to stop relying on you, and as a result your untrustworthiness increases greatly.

"Truth is the cry of all, but the game of few," said lawyer and renown French playwright Tristan Bernard. Your words represent you, even more so today, when so much is done online and through text and misinterpretations are rampant. The importance of words are often dismissed as 'oh you misunderstood,' 'I didn't mean that,' 'that's not what I said,' or 'forget that, it'll blow over when you focus on my next thought.' However, what you say and how you say it—then not living up to that, or backtracking or embellishing—is often the root of countless problems.

Many people have difficulty saying no to those they like or those they don't want to disappoint. However, it is far better to say no than to say yes and either not be able to live up to that commitment (which creates a greater disappointment) or to build silent resentment for having committed to something you really couldn't or didn't want to do—remember the unsaid is felt and body language does not go unnoticed. Over time these silent demons build up.

When you don't say what you mean, difficulties arise. This includes not speaking up when you need to. Not saying something also conveys a message; saying nothing can just as easily create misunderstandings or implied meanings. How true are you to your word?

Your Relationships

Relationships are like food and air. We need them to

survive. We do not live in a vacuum, nor can we sustain life in one. We are social animals and much of our motivation comes from our relationships. Better health is directly linked to healthy relationships, just as illness is exacerbated by poor or toxic relationships. Children fare far better with a healthy single parent than being subject to parents in a toxic marriage. Also, when our relationships disintegrate or when we find ourselves without them, loneliness sets in. Loneliness is a major factor in depression, illness, and a shorter life span. That alone tells us that the way we connect with each other is vital to the quality of our lives. The COVID-19 pandemic has illustrated not only our interconnectedness, but our need for one another as well. We all experience loneliness sometime in our lives; it's a normal part of the ebb and flow of our existence and our connections. The question is, how long do you let loneliness go on before taking action to move on and remedy the situation?

Consider the relationships in your life. Which ones are the most important to you? Why? Most people think they must include their closest blood relatives, parents, siblings, and children. However, if we are honest, some of those are not always the most important relationships to us, and some are not necessarily relationships that serve us well. Sometimes, those related to you are not the ones closest or most supportive of you. They are not necessarily the ones that know you best or call you out and stand by you when it's critical. Only you know who those people are in your life. Examine each relationship without the labels associated with their role in your life and make your determination based on connection, intimacy, support, honesty, and loyalty.

What do the relationships in your life look like? Are they contentious? Superficial? Argumentative? Bland? Trustworthy? Loving? Full of jealousy? We all have some form of each of these in our lives, but the question is what is the overriding tone of our relationships? Do you have healthy relationships? Which ones are healthy, which ones are not, and which ones are questionable? Your relationships tell you about yourself. Healthy relationships allow two people to be mutually honest about their struggles and to seek mutual accountability and encouragement from each other. Do you expect help and support from your friends and family and complain when they don't give it to you, and then when they ask for your support, you don't give it either? Why would you expect them to support and help you if you are not willing to do the same?

Communication is paramount to a healthy, solid relationship of any kind. Miscommunication is the frontrunner for a majority of problems. Poor communication can result in misunderstandings, fear, anxiety, frustration, and feelings of separateness because someone isn't feeling understood. Also, a lack of communication can result in denial and passive-aggressive behaviors. Are you a good communicator?

Our younger generations have grown up with social media and personal technology as part of their lives, and many older generations have also taken to this technology wholeheartedly. This has both positive and negative affects. On the positive side, we can stay connected more easily (email, text, WhatsApp, Facebook, Twitter, Instagram) which allows us to glimpse into lives we may not otherwise get glimpses into—from other cultures and social strata—and that can bridge certain bias gaps. However, as we have seen, this can also widen those gaps through manipulation. What happens if most of your communication happens via technology? What does it do to the quality of communication, to intimacy, to real connection, and to a person's ability to communicate and to relate face-to-face and out in the world? Is something lost or missing?

Albert Mehrabian, a pioneer researcher of body language in the 1950s, found that the total impact of a message is about seven percent verbal (conveyed through words), 38 percent through certain vocal elements (including tone of voice, inflection, and other sounds), and 55 percent through things such as facial expressions, gestures, and postures. How effectively can you experience complete communication through sound bites via text, email, Twitter, or Facebook? That communication is mostly informational and largely one way. FaceTime, Zoom, and Skype are better, but nuances can still be lost. That is why so much disappointment can come from relying on relationships that have developed over the Internet. When you finally meet, in person, the individual you've been communicating with through an electronic channel, and encounter the reality of your assumptions, the results can vary greatly from what you expected.

Words can be used to confuse and intimidate, to clarify and connect, and to embolden and inspire; however, you can miss much of the intent if there is no personal element along with it. Certain cultures won't even entertain the notion of beginning a business relationship (let alone a personal one) without first meeting face-to-face. True connection happens in person. Your life happens in person.

Do you share meals with the people with whom you are in relationships? Sitting around and 'breaking bread' is a bonding experience. It's a time you can share and focus on each other without distraction. This means engaging face-to-face—without electronics. This is how we show that we are listening and involved in each other's lives—by being present with each other.

My spouse and I were with friends at a restaurant one May evening and we were at a table next to a longer one where a group of elegantly dressed teenagers were being seated. I quickly realized that it was prom night for them. At one point during the evening, I looked over at the table of young people and was struck by what I saw: all of the girls sat on one side of the table and all of the guys on the other, and every one of them, with the exception of the few that had gone to the restroom, had their phones in their hands and was either texting or checking messages. When one of them would speak to the other, they wouldn't look at that person, instead they would glance up and then return their gaze to their phone. That was a disturbing image and it made me wonder if these young people knew how to relate to each other without their phones or some kind of crutch in the mix.

The dynamics of intimate relationships are the deepest and most potentially volatile associations in which we can see ourselves. It is in this playground that we encounter the best and worst of who we are. In the midst of intimacy, we have opportunities to find ourselves.

"Relationships are like pressures that push you in thirty-six directions of the compass. But, as in a crowded streetcar, if you learn how to maintain your balance against all the weights, you might arrive at yourself," said novelist Diana Chang in *The Frontiers of Love*.

People naturally seek to love and be loved. There exists in

each of us a burning desire to do or to be. For some it is a blinding, all-consuming craving; for others it lies buried under the rubble of emotional scars. Most of us have felt the scars of love's growing pains. If you find yourself in the place of pain surrounding love, allow yourself to feel it. Embrace it and, when you truly do, you will shine a light upon yourself and make unexpected discoveries. You may find that the intimate relationship brings up old wounds more intensely and that it brings to the surface emotions you may have thought you were done with. The intensity of feelings within the intimate relationship are designed to assist you to get a deeper look within. Lay them bare for yourself, allow yourself to be vulnerable and use those feelings as a way to grow yourself toward the highest vision of yourself.

Do you have expectations of yourself or of whom you should be with? Are you impatient that your life doesn't look a certain way, a way that you believe it needs to look? Are you anxious and constantly seeking someone to fill the void? Are you jealous? If your answer to any of these questions is "yes" then you are human, and perhaps a shift of perspective would be helpful to end your anxiety. Consider that who and where you are is exactly the place from which to fully accept yourself and to allow yourself to let go of the judgment and anxiety that either you or your life doesn't look a certain way. It is not easy to let go; but once it is done, all else becomes easier. If you find yourself getting jealous of someone or something, consider this: There are times when you're ahead, there are times when you're behind, but the race is long and in the end, the race is only with yourself.

Let go of the tightness in your stomach, of the ache in your shoulders, of the racing and the chatter in your mind, of the clouds in your eyes, of the fears in your bones—and reach for the hopes of your heart and the reality of where you stand now. Acknowledge your circumstances, then look at your dreams regardless of your starting point. Make an honest assessment of what has been working and what hasn't. Commit to pursuing change where change is necessary. With this release, the direction of your pursuit becomes clear and love can find you.

Every relationship comes with certain agreements. There are implied agreements inherent to certain types of relationships such as parent and child, where the implied social agreement is that the parent will sustain, nurture, and protect the child up to a certain age. Another example is the broad agreement between employer and employee where the implication is that the employer dictates the parameters around a particular job and provides a value exchange for the work performed. There are also specifically negotiated agreements, both verbal and written. Some basic examples of written contracts are real estate purchases, executive employment contracts, service and vendor proposals, pre-nuptial agreements, manufacturing contracts, and countless others.

Marriage is complex blend of agreements. First, marriage is a legal and binding contract and all that comes with it, such as community property and parental rights, unless specifically outlined differently in a separate contract (a pre-nuptial), which could be a small or substantial written document. Second, once you are married, there is an implied social contract. And third, there are usually verbal contracts between the couple that are as distinct and individual as they are.

In all cases, an agreement is a commitment. Do you keep your commitments? The most important agreements you will make are with yourself. If you commit to being true to your word, but frequently find an excuse for why you couldn't be true to it one time or not in certain situations, then you will likely find yourself in problematic situations throughout areas of your life.

Reflections:

1. Think about the people you spend the most time with. Are they supportive of you? Could and would you turn to them for help? If not, why not? Are you there for them in the same way?

2. Do you see yourself as successful? Why or why not? What do you wish was different about you? Why? What areas do you excel in?

3. Think about one time you did not fulfill a promised obligation. Why did that happen? How did you feel about it?

4. Think of a time when a friend didn't live up to their promise to you? How did it make you feel? How did you react?

5. Do you always mean what you say? When do you not? Why?

Chapter Six

WHO WANTS TO BE ACCOUNTABLE?

How you do anything is how you do everything. Accountability is the bridge to character. For most people, the word accountability has a negative association. In the dictionary the definition is: Responsibility, liability, and answerability. When someone asks if you are the one accountable for something, do you assume that if you say yes you will be in trouble? We have become masters at passing the buck to protect our jobs, our reputations, our relationships, or whatever it is that we may be afraid of risking. We are happy to be accountable when we are sure that it will result in praise, but loathe to risk it when the result may be crisis, requesting us to adjust or change, or failure. It's fear that prevents us from owning our opinions and our actions. What this behavior has created is people who don't stand for anything, who are apathetic, fearful, and ultimately ineffective. Blaming others, circumstances or the weather is not the mark of a leader or even the mark of someone effective at navigating their own life.

Shonda Rhimes created a show called *How To Get Away With Murder*. The culture and the concept of the show is anti-accountability.

This creates an environment of obstacles, conflict, and anxiety that is great for drama, but not good for real life. Denying, manipulating, and covering up creates more problems, not solutions. Do you ever really "get away" with anything? It may appear that you got away with not getting caught stealing, or you got away with that thing on your resume that isn't true, or that lie, or any countless number of things. But, you always know what you did or didn't do or what you know or don't know, even if others don't. You have to live with that knowledge and it will seep out in ways throughout your life you may not even be aware of. It will subtly and subconsciously inform your attitudes, beliefs, and actions going forward. My spouse always says, "Wherever you go, you take yourself with you." So, the answer is no, you ultimately don't 'get away' with things.

There is a difference between responsibility and accountability. Responsibility is learning to choose effective behaviors in order to live up to your commitments. Accountability is owning the consequences of your choices. A more comprehensive definition comes from Steve and Jill Morris, who have a company called ChoiceWorks. Their work on accountability is extraordinary with proven results. They define accountability as: owning the consequences of our choices in delivering the agreed-to results.

What does owning mean? Owning means that you bear the responsibility for the consequences that may result from what you think and do. Ownership creates opportunity. This means that you own your choices. Everyday events occur that require you to make a continuous stream of decisions, from the smallest ones— should you sit or stand, brush your teeth, drink this or that—to the big ones such as moving, getting married, changing jobs. Every choice you make has some effect. Both thoughts and actions create subsequent outcomes.

If the reason you fear owning one of your behaviors is because you feel it is not perfect or you are ashamed in some way, understand that we all suffer from feeling inadequate at times and have various forms of insecurities and vulnerabilities. Not a single one of us achieves perfection in all things, if ever. It's a construct of judgment and comparison. Let go of the notion of perfection and inadequacy when looking within for what's morally correct. This is where character is built.

Thoughts put you in certain frames of mind to assist you in processing information or learning and strategizing. Actions put those thoughts in motion and lead to results. That is the second part of the definition—the consequences of your choices.

Thinking you are not making a decision by putting off saying yes or no, or delaying a decision are decisions. Believing that you are absolved from accountability by saying that you never made your choice is not a valid excuse. Not making a choice is a choice. It's a cop-out that plays to your weaknesses, not to your strengths. Being accountable for a bad decision is a sign of a stronger character than turning away from your accountability by claiming it wasn't your decision because you failed to make one.

Pointing the finger at someone or something else and not owning your choices is the behavior of a victim. Victims think other people and situations cause their choices. They blame everything 'out there' for the things that are wrong in their lives. They don't see that they are choosing—making the choices that lead them to their circumstances.

Things may happen in your environment that are beyond your control. However, you are responsible for choosing your attitude in every situation, even the most horrific ones. The alternative is to become animalistic and ruled by your basest unbridled impulses and emotions, reacting without thought and becoming a victim of circumstance. You have the power to choose how you interpret what you see, hear, touch, taste, smell, and think. You always make the choice in how you perceive something.

After 'owning the consequences of your choices,' the last part of the definition is 'agreed-to results.' Every action has a result. The goal of the action you take is the desired result. You want a chair in the corner, you take action to carry and place it there. And, since we are interdependent on each other, we make both implicit and explicit agreements to function in any kind of relationship environment. If your boss asks you to create a budget and it is part of the job that you agreed to, then the action you must take is to create, write up, and hand over a budget. If you and your lover agree not to date other people and you are asked to go out on a date with someone else, your action must be to turn them down or to re-negotiate with your lover if you are to adhere to the agreed-to results. If you rent an apartment and agree to the amount of the rent to be paid on a specific timetable, you must pay that rent in accordance with those terms if you are to remain happily in that apartment. If you choose an action that would create a different result from the one agreed to, then you must own and be prepared to be accountable for the consequences of that action. We all know that cheating on your lover would cause an upheaval in the relationship if fidelity were agreed to and your partner found out.

They may leave you or the relationship would take a different turn.

Accountability begins with being accountable to yourself first. It also begins with a commitment to taking responsibility for all of your choices. Accountable people are proactive. People of great character are accountable. Take an honest assessment of yourself and notice where you may not be accountable to yourself. In what areas of life are you reactive rather than proactive? Do you look for whom you can blame when something goes wrong? If you don't know what to do, do you ask for help or do the research to find out, or do you throw up your hands and wait for someone else to do it, or for events to happen to you? Are you a problem solver or a complainer?

If you are not accountable to yourself, yet insist and attempt to hold others accountable, you become a bully. When you commit to being accountable to yourself, you also commit to allowing others to hold you accountable. If we wish to create a culture of accountability we need to understand this. And, if this understanding is to be enforced, we must learn to communicate clearly with each other in an environment where open dialogue is encouraged without blame or name-calling. There is a difference between calling someone out (holding them accountable) to point out an inconsistency in their agreements and what has recently been deemed 'calling out' as a way to shine a spotlight on some political incorrectness based on a subjective viewpoint. The latter is meant to shame rather than invoke meaningful discourse and this is not about accountability. This kind of behavior is a virtue signaling to your political side or 'tribe' to gain praise and assurance that you are still a part of those views, whether they are right or wrong.

Enabling bad behavior (shaming is also bad behavior) is the

opposite of accountability. Many people enable those they love because they are afraid of conflict or rejection. This helps neither the loved one nor the enabler and disintegrates deeper and deeper into unhealthy relationships.

If you don't hold people accountable, they know it and they don't take the agreements they have with you seriously. Just as you won't take seriously someone else's rules if they seem not to care about enforcing them. Holding people accountable takes courage. When someone fails to come through on what they agreed to, immediately call them out on it by asking them questions such as: "What was your intention when you agreed to this? What happened? What do you expect to result from not doing it? What impact do you think it has on me?" Don't ask why they didn't do what they agreed to because that only generates excuses and can lead the conversation down a rabbit hole. If they don't have a grasp of the consequences, explain it to them in detail. This is uncomfortable, but leads to resolution. There has to be a cost to the other person if they don't take their agreements seriously. The cost can be as small as the discomfort of being confronted and asked to self-evaluate to the cost of greater consequences.

In business, the more specific and clear both your written and verbal agreements are the less room there is for confusion and misunderstanding. It's always best to have your base agreement in writing, that way you both have a document to refer to should a disagreement arise. In dealing with day-to-day tasks, many partners use email as a way to ensure clarity and commitment. When you agree to something in writing, even a simple 'yes I will handle that' in an email, it creates a way to hold each other accountable to an agreement. Where most people fail in partnerships is in making assumptions that the other person knows what they mean or is agreeing to the same terms without having to make it specific. Specificity is very important. We all operate on different time tables and have our own unique ways of processing information. Making an assumption about what your partner thinks about a task or a project and that they feel the same sense of urgency as you do can be a big mistake if you don't confirm those thoughts and timetables in advance.

Marriage can be a minefield in navigating accountability issues, particularly because of miscommunication. In some marriages, the couple specifically agrees to certain responsibilities, while others are implied. Often, what happens in a marriage is that the more one partner remembers the tasking details of day-to-day life, the less the other remembers. For example, let's say Janet worries about money, about the kids, about what Jack needs to be doing around the house and to keep his health in check. The more Janet worries about these things, the less Jack worries. The more she worries about his time away from their relationship, the less Jack even notices that it's happening. Whatever she worries about, Jack will naturally compensate by being less worried. This is the nature of partnerships. John Gray, relationship counselor and author of the Mars and Venus series of books says, "If a man misplaces his keys and his wife always knows where they are, his tendency to feel responsible for remembering where they are will decrease. He will actually start to forget them more often instead of simply assigning a spot and always putting them there."

How do you handle a situation where this kind of compensation is happening? Complaining to your partner or berating or nagging them doesn't work; it actually creates more problems. The last thing anyone responds to well is being put down. Berating someone or saying things like "you said you would do this, but you never do," "you're always late," or "you never pick up after yourself," doesn't promote accountability; it promotes defensiveness and anger. Even if that's not your intent, the way you deliver your message can create a clear understanding with the other person or a defensive reaction because they are feeling attacked. The most effective shifts begin in the moment. Let's say Jack forgets where his keys are, Janet should pause, prepare him on how to remember where he put them (have him retrace his movements from when he had them last, consider having him pick a spot that would be convenient for him to put them both coming and going), and persist in allowing him to remember and find his keys on his own. The more she repeats this, the quicker Jack will simply begin remembering on his own because the role will become his. Clear, consistent communication is a key component to holding others accountable and to your own willingness to be held accountable.

I want to take a moment to make a comment about judgment. There is a huge difference between judging someone and holding them accountable. Judgment is a form of defense against our own feelings of not being enough. When you judge someone, you are making a form of comparison, placing blame or saying that they are somehow lesser than you based on a certain behavior. This is becoming common in our political discourse. We all have a tendency to judge and in some situations judgment is called for, while in others, it can be misguided. When I catch myself judging someone,

I make an attempt to look at why I'm reacting so strongly and where my own vulnerability lies and if there's something I need to do regarding accountability—either mine or the other person's. In one instance, I was furious with someone for not doing some agreed upon actions. We wrote up a contract clearly outlining each of our tasks and they failed to do theirs. I let it fester for months, feeling hostile and judging that person in my head, believing they were messed up or incapable. When I calmly sat down and examined the entire situation, I realized that I was really mad at myself, because I failed to hold them accountable each time they failed to live up to what they said they would do. I allowed their excuses to stand, hoping that it would magically change. It didn't change anywhere along the way, and I was left with knowing that I did not do what I promised myself I would do, hold them accountable the first time they broke our agreement, first by talking to them and pointing it out and seeing if we needed to renegotiate, or abandon that agreement and then make my own assessment of where I needed to be within that relationship.

Reflections:

1.   *Think of someone you consider to be a bully. What trait do they have? Do they accept responsibility for their own actions?*

2.   *Recall an example when you reacted to something without thinking, because it made you mad, or triggered you in some way. What happened after you reacted that way? How did you feel? How*

would the situation have been different if you had taken a moment to think before reacting?

3.   Consider an incident when you were pro-active. What happened? How did you feel about your choices and reactions, then? How about now, in retrospect?

4.   Think of someone in your life who consistently blames others for things that are wrong in their life or workplace? Do you respect them? Why or why not?

5.   When and under what circumstances did you last judge someone? Were you ever judged unfairly? How did you react?

Chapter Seven

WHO DO YOU WANT TO BE?

Self-awareness is the basic foundation for self-acceptance and self confidence. The more you know and understand yourself, your motivations, your capabilities, your lacks, who you are, and why and how you think and feel the way you do, the more capable you are of making better decisions in every area of your life and of growing into the person closest to whom you ideally want to be.

Having an idea of how you come across to others is a part of this examination. The image people have of you is the first thing that comes to mind when they think of you. The way you come across to others is a combination of numerous components, including your appearance, your cleanliness, your inner energy, the way you carry yourself, your attitude, your receptivity, your demeanor, your tone, your ability to engage in conversation or not, the way you move, and more.

Most people think that you have to be a certain kind of physically attractive being to rank at the top of the food chain. However, the old saying that beauty is in the eye of the beholder is quite true, for there are as many kinds of attractive as there are people and, what you find attractive, someone else may not. Attractiveness is subjective. You should note that your physical attractiveness is not as important as the energy you project from within.

Certain factors rank more than physical attractiveness in what you project to the outside world. Some of those are: 1) Cleanliness and good grooming habits—this tells others that you care about hygiene and yourself and that they can get close to you without fearing contagion. 2) Eye contact when speaking to a person—this subconsciously communicates that you are self assured, willing to connect, and don't have anything to hide. 3) Posture—informs your level of self confidence. Self confidence comes across with power. Poor posture, not looking people in the eye, and a fickle attitude tend to connote frailty. 4) Your demeanor—lets people know if you are overly aggressive, timid, willing to engage, open, secretive, and so on.

In defining a picture for yourself of how others see you, you may want to begin with some basic questions: Do you stick with what you believe or do you constantly try to please everybody else? This speaks to your self-confidence and ability to remain true to who you are.

Do you look people in the eye when you speak to them? This is a sign of being present, engaging, and connecting. Are you present when interacting with others or are you looking around, at your phone, fiddling with an object, or thinking of something else? This lack of presence shows a disrespect to the persons you're with and is always noted by their subconscious.

Are you a good listener or are you too concerned with what you're going to say to really hear the other person? Being a good listener encourages trust.

Do you have a mind-set that you are willing to learn and grow or that you already know everything? Are you defensive? None of us know it all and that type of attitude can be off-putting, even when you think it should be a strength at times, such as in a job interview. Being a "know-it-all" actually works to the contrary. This doesn't mean to shy away from what you do know—absolutely not. This means that you should be willing to learn about what you do not know and to be open to looking at different perspectives.

Are you worried about what people think or are you comfortable in your own skin? This is an area that requires a delicate balance. Being comfortable in who you are is vital, yet some people mistake it for arrogance or bullying, which are two different things. If you care about others and about creating an atmosphere of mutual regard, your comfort will naturally come across without a need to force your views.

Are you willing to hear helpful, positive criticism? When you hear a note of criticism toward you, as a first reaction try to pay attention rather than take offense. If you are told something critical about yourself once, note it, think about it, and it may very well be it has no bearing on you and was a result of someone else's "stuff." If you hear the same thing twice, really examine it and be on the lookout for what may have brought it about. If you hear the same thing from three or more sources, take serious stock in it and ask yourself the hard questions about whether they may be right and how you can correct whatever it is if you feel that their observation is something you don't wish to embody.

Your reputation is part of your image. Are you someone who disappears from your friends when they are going through a crisis?

Or are you there to help them through? When a friend has a success, do you celebrate their success or do you turn away and minimize it? Are you jealous of their successes? Are you courageous in your own affairs or do you buckle under pressure? When you say you will do something, do you follow through, or do you drop the ball? Can people count on you when you agree to something? Are you hot-tempered? Or passive-aggressive? Or passive? Are you easily led? Do you always insist on getting your way? It takes a lifetime to build a reputation, but mere minutes to destroy it. Your choices matter. The now infamous Penn State football coach Joe Paterno made a choice to look the other way regarding Jerry Sandinsky's abuse of young boys, and at the end of a sixty-one year career, when his choice came to light, he was fired in disgrace. That one decision, thinking it wasn't his responsibility because he didn't know for sure and didn't want to know or listen and try to know, cost him a lifetime of legacy.

Having an awareness of how you come across gives you the opportunity to adjust and to avoid miscommunication and misunderstandings with others. This allows you to get better results in achieving your goals.

Now that I've got you thinking about who you are, the next step is to ask if you currently embody the highest vision of yourself—the person you are most proud to be. I believe that just as the way we innovate and improve our world, we always have room for improvement within. Perfection is illusive and the only sure thing is change. Life is fluid, and motion is what makes it exciting, challenging, and beautiful. If our lives were static, we would very likely be bored and may as well have stayed in caves. Nothing in existence remains exactly the same from one day to the next. That's both the challenge and the beauty. After all, if you're not growing, you're dying.

As a culture, we have become people who identify with what we have rather than with who we are. In the film *Lucy*, Scarlett Johansson plays a character who begins using a larger and larger percentage of her brain. One of her first insights is that we as humans are more concerned with wanting than with being which is contributing to our downfall.

Materialism has created an overwhelming overabundance of non-essential junk that has depleted our resources and filled our landfills. For what? The short, fleeting moments of instant gratification that are quickly forgotten in search of the next thing. Some of us just keep purchasing and accumulating. Hoarding is a modern day phenomenon. Few of us truly treasure and genuinely appreciate what we have. We don't take time to admire and to save up for something that is of lasting quality and that we will then value and take pleasure in for years. Most of us purchase things, then throw them out when they're broken or we tire of them and re-purchase something in its place. When a perfectly good and not very old appliance or camera breaks, we don't fix it. We've made it more economical to just buy a new one and throw out the old one. Think about the values we are creating with this type of behavior. Think about the fact that we are placing a premium on superficiality. We judge someone by the stuff they have and the more they have the easier it is for us to overlook bad behavior. When someone is a genuine, for lack of a better word, asshole, we tend to overlook it if that person is wealthy.

A 2017 Gallup Poll said that 85 percent of adults are not happy and actually hate their jobs. That figure has not changed much over the years. Considering that they spend the majority of their lives doing their jobs, this is a hugely sad state of affairs. It's fair to say that we all would like to be happy in our lives in whatever way we each define that.

Do you simply wish to get well paid for what you're good at and enjoy doing? The world would be a saner and more peaceful place if we all did just that. Unfortunately, the formula for achievement gets buried in a myriad of political and emotional landscapes that lead most people to disillusionment. You don't have to be one of them.

Our drive for fame, wanting the next fad, and instant gratification can distract us from managing our inner life. This drive for instant gratification can be damaging to our soul. A drive for success can be healthy when combined with self-understanding. I want to talk about the notion of fame as celebrity in contrast to the notion of being successful at something. Success is something you earn. Celebrity happens to you. There's a big difference. Success comes as a result of accomplishment and achievements, where celebrity happens out of popularity in the moment. Success can be lasting and fulfilling, because once you've achieved something it becomes a part of your history, a part of who you are, and no one can take that away from you. The road to your achievements is filled with experience, which in turn builds your knowledge and your capacity to grow and to achieve even more. Oprah, Nikola Tesla, and Stephen Hawking are examples of such success. They earned it, putting in the work and the hours necessary to rise above the others in their field. Vincent Van Gogh never had fame during his lifetime, but his achievements earned him a legacy of honor, respect, and esteem.

Celebrity, on the other hand, is fleeting, moody, unpredictable, and empty. And is something that can be taken away from you on a whim. so depending on it for any kind of satisfaction can be hugely disillusioning. Ask those who've only had celebrity without real achievement. Why are so many of us obsessed with having our "fifteen minutes of fame"? When you look closely, you realize that it's an illusion, a trap, and a distraction from a happy and healthy life. It is a gratification solely for your ego, not for your soul. Success takes work and experience in anything you want to be good at. If you don't succeed immediately, keep going, because most people simply give up and some give up right before they would have made it.

The amount of time you spend doing what you want to be good at is critical. Writer and scholar Daniel Levin, who has done numerous studies on the topic, says "The emerging picture from such studies is that ten thousand hours of practice is required to achieve the level associated with being a world-class expert—in anything. In study after study, of composers, basketball players, fiction writers, ice skaters, concert pianists, chess players, master criminals, and what have you, this number comes up again and again. Of course, this doesn't address why some people get more out of their practice sessions than others do. But no one has yet found a case in which true world-class experience was accomplished in less time. It seems that it takes the brain this long to assimilate all that it needs to know to achieve true mastery."

In the book *Outliers,* Malcom Gladwell shows how some of the most successful people in the world all put in their ten thousand hours before rising to the top, including The Beatles and even Mozart, who was considered a child prodigy.

Einstein said, "Failure is success in progress." In today's age of instant gratification, it can be difficult to grasp that it takes time and failure along the way to get good at something. Even at being the person you want to be on an inner level. In order for a tree to grow tall and strong it must first develop the unseen roots that will hold it up, yet most of us admire the leaves, flowers, and branches without thinking much about the tree's roots. We do the same with people and often ourselves. Part of the problem is the focus on our outer lives at the expense of our inner ones. You can choose to take control of your inner life first, put in the time, and the rest will follow.

Actor/Comedian/Writer and Director Tom Shadyac, known for films such as *Ace Ventura: Pet Detective, Liar Liar, Patch Adams,* and more, had an accident that put him in a coma and which caused him to re-evaluate a few things. He then made a film called *I AM* where he explored what's wrong with our world and how we can improve both it and the way we live in it. Shadyac made this film in pursuit of truth. He said, "As early as I can remember I simply wanted to know what was true, and somehow I perceived at a very early age that what I was being taught was not the whole truth and nothing but the truth....What I discovered, when I began to look deeply, was that the world I was living in was a lie.

"Much to my surprise, the accumulation of material wealth was a neutral phenomenon, neither good or bad, and certainly did not buy happiness." In searching for the answers to what's wrong in our world, he said, "I didn't want to hear the usual answers, like war, hunger, poverty, the environmental crisis, or even greed. These are not the problems; they are the symptoms of a larger endemic problem. In *I AM*, I wanted to talk about the root cause of the ills of the world, because if there is a common cause, and we can talk about it, air it out in a public forum, then we have a chance to solve it." One of the things he learned is that in some native cultures extreme materialism is equated with insanity. Tom's exploration led him to leave the film industry, sell his mansion in Los Angeles, move into a smaller place, give a good bulk of his money to causes he believed in, and begin teaching. His focusing on his inner life led him to a path of greater joy for himself. He said, "What was happening to me was definitely on the inside. But after I gave up everything I felt a lot more joy in my life. A lot more contentment. There's nothing wrong, though, with making a lot of money...this is not a judgment on anyone at all. I was just taking in a lot more than I needed and this wasn't good for me."

I ask you to take control of your inner life. The person who can't decide what it is they want, who has no goal, whose thoughts are filled with confusion, and who relies on others or certain circumstances to point them in a direction, winds up creating a life of frustration, anxiety, and worry for themselves. If you do not know who you want to be, let alone who you are, you are at the mercy and whims of others. You are reactive and not creating the life you are capable of creating for yourself, and chances are you are unhappy.

When you operate at a reactive level you are not being authentic. Authenticity requires a certain degree of vulnerability as well as self-awareness. Singer Alicia Keys talks about when she was discovered. She says, "I didn't want to be all dressed up, all made up—I wanted to be myself, which hadn't been done before. People fell in love with the real me, and I still feel blessed that that was how the journey began."

Just as we filter the variables in any given situation, we do the same with people. Your authenticity is what people instinctively pick up on in the first encounter. If you mask who you really are, you are merely prolonging the game of the ultimate reveal. Some people make it a lifetime habit and wonder why the things they want to happen don't or not in the way that ultimately suits them or brings them any joy.

This quote by author Jack London is one of my favorites: "I would rather be ashes than dust! I would rather that my spark should burn out in a brilliant blaze than it should be stifled by dry rot. I would rather be a superb meteor, every atom of me in magnificent glow, than a sleepy and permanent planet. The proper function of man is to live, not to exist. I shall not waste my days in trying to prolong them. I shall use my time."

You can't have what you desire until you're clear about what that is. People who aren't living the life they say they wish for or have some of the things they say they desire could be because when you strip away the material items from their list, they aren't clear and/or don't know what they really yearn for in the bigger picture. The confusion can come in the form of two conflicts: 1) What you really want vs. what you think you want and 2) What you really want vs. what you think you should want. In addition to those conflicts, another can rear its ugly head from the subconscious— guilt—creating more problems. Guilt over having a desire and shame around not achieving it leads to excuses, rationalizations and defensiveness, or denial.

Before you start listing the things you desire, ask yourself first what kind of life you want to live. Are you a person who wants to engage in and be a part of bigger things, or someone who is an observer? Are you compelled to create or are you more content being a support person or doing analysis? Do you prefer routine or get excited by an ever-changing landscape? Are you a problem solver or organizer? There are dozens of questions to begin with on a very basic level, but then you must apply your inner values to give them dimension. There are hundreds of questions to ask yourself to build an inner foundation that will support your desires.

First, allow yourself to explore your values. You can begin with the following questions:

1. What are some of the life challenges, hardships, issues, obstacles, and pain you have faced?

2. Which of these were you able to overcome?

3. How did you overcome them?

4. Why were you able to overcome them?

5. How did you achieve what you consider your greatest successes?

6. What are some activities that make your heart sing?

7. If money were not an issue, what would you want to do with your time?

8. If you could affect change in the world, what would you most want to do?

Below is a list of values. Pick the top five and rank them in order of priority of what's most important to you. Add to this list or create your own if you need to.

Security	Time freedom	Financial freedom
Love	Challenge	Adventure
Passion	Intimacy	Comfort
Productivity	Environment	Beauty
Success	Giving/Service	Friends
Family	Primary relationship	Respect
Integrity	Achievement	Being the best
Intelligence	Health	Fitness
Honesty	Joy	Play
Inner peace	Courage	Empowerment
Learning	Spirituality	Independence
Creativity	Personal growth	Leadership

Accept who you are, the circumstances you find yourself in, and the choices you have made thus far, without judgment, and proceed from there. Be honest with yourself. Look back only to access that which will assist you going forward.

We each move through our lives in our unique rhythms. Your rhythm is as individual as your fingerprint. A piece of music has its own melody and, while two musical pieces may share the same beat, the same chords, the same key, how they are put together is what distinguishes one from another. Rhythm is defined as a strong, regular, repeated pattern of movement and sound. It comes from the idea 'to flow.'

Each person's life flows in a particular way. We can see patterns, routines, habits, pace, levels of energy, and more. We are each motivated by different factors. Our drive comes from varying sources. What you consider fun may not be what others consider fun. What you may consider easy, others may find to be a struggle. People have different sleep patterns, energy levels, physical features and capabilities, likes, dislikes, emotional capacities, tolerances, joys, and fears. This is what makes life interesting, exciting, and challenging. We all have something that makes us distinctively ourselves as individuals. The content and successful people learn not only to embrace their unique rhythm and to use it effectively in their lives but they also find a way to surround themselves with those who harmonize with their rhythm, not those who silence it. Trying to conform to something that doesn't fit who you truly are doesn't serve you or those for whom you are doing the conforming in the long run.

Getting in touch with your rhythm comes from knowing yourself. If you feel that you don't know what your rhythm is, then you may not consciously be aware of it, but intuitively you know what makes your spirit sing—what makes you feel the most alive, effective, productive, and relevant. Delve into that feeling. Explore that place and what you can do with it. Bring it forward to create the kind of person you wish to be.

Think about who you want to be, what you want your life to look like, and what you want to be doing on a daily basis, then write it down. Read it every day until you can't not think that that is who you are, and you begin to see pieces of the life you desire. If you find yourself thinking of yourself or your life other than in ways you want to be, stop. Stop and rethink. Remember, your world begins with your thoughts. If you succumb to seeing yourself as a victim, you continue to reinforce that in your life. Your thoughts are powerful. Negative visions of yourself, your circumstances, and your future set you back.

Once you develop an awareness of your thoughts and begin cultivating the ones that best serve you, the next step is your word—what you say.

Your choice of words and how they are administered are critical to your effectiveness in being understood. Your words are the first step in revealing who you are to the rest of us. Take time every day to put down your phone, turn off your computer and tablet, and personally engage with the people and the world around you.

If you want people to understand you, speak with clarity, ask questions if something seems off, and be open to others questioning you. Be consistent in what you say. Your consistency will inform and reinforce who you say you are.

If you want people to consider that you are true to your word, then be careful how and when you give it, no matter how small the matter. If you say you will take out the trash, then take out the trash. If you say you will stop by after the meeting, then do that or, if something prevents it, then at least call to acknowledge that you made the commitment and now need to change it. However, it's better not to make commitments you can't live up to than to go back on your word.

The next step is action. Examine your behavior on a daily basis. Take note of how you do the simple things in your life and see if they are a microcosmic representation of the larger things in your life, such as certain lacks, problems, or issues you are having. Then change those actions. People are creatures of habit. Sir Isaac Newton's law of inertia says that a body in motion tends to remain in motion unless acted upon by an outside force. In other words, the more you keep doing what you are doing, the more you will get what you've got. Based on who you want to be, engage in actions that reflect that person. And remember, how you do anything is how you do everything.

You can't have what you seek until you're clear about what that is. I'm deliberately staying away from the word 'want.' The word 'want' itself implies lack. One definition of the word is to feel the lack of something, another is to feel the need for something, and the third is to feel a desire for something. I'd like to focus on the third since it's the most positive and can compel you into action. It is true that you need to identify your desire before you can bring it about. American baseball player Branch Rickey said that luck is the residue of design. You can put yourself on the right path as you know it to be at the time—the design. But there are certain things you cannot establish. This is where luck comes into play. You cannot know the exact road that you will take to get there or what it will look like, nor the details of what you will encounter along the way. You may even detour from your original desire if another overriding desire takes over and nullifies the original one. The one thing you can control is your inner world. Your inner world creates your outer world and making changes to your inner world is the greatest victory that often goes unrecognized.

The foundation for clearing the path to your desires lies in the more foundational question of who you want to be. How would you like yourself, others, and your children to think of you? Begin with the inner work first.

What do you think people would say about you after you're gone? What would you like them to say? This is a good place to begin determining who you want to be. You may consider doing an exercise where you write your own eulogy and see what comes up. Think about the following questions: What qualities will people most remember about you? What kinds of accomplishments will they honor? What truth will they reveal about you? How have you affected or changed peoples lives? Who are the people remembering you?

It's human nature to want to be remembered, to feel important and useful, and to leave some sort of footprint on the world. If you're a parent, you may think of your children as the footprint you leave behind. Even with that, you, like many others, want to see a broader, more individual impact.

As you think about the footprint you wish to leave, consider that whatever you confidently expect of yourself and your life becomes your own self-fulfilling prophecy.

Reflections:

1. What is something that you do or put off doing that you know you should be doing differently, but tell yourself, that either it doesn't matter, or you'll get to it eventually? What if you did it differently?

2. Is there something you believe you are talented at or an expert on, but you can't seem to advance? How much time have you and do you spend cultivating or practicing that?

3. List three ways you want to be remembered. What behaviors are you practicing regularly to make that happen?

4. Ask three trusted friends to pick three words that encapsulate who they think you are.

Chapter Eight

GETTING FROM A TO B

Your Comfort Zone

How many people do you know that say they want to do something, anything, but never get to it? Years go by and they haven't done it, or even taken a step towards it. Most of us recognize a part of ourselves in that kind of procrastination in some area of our lives. How and why does that happen? Sometimes it happens because, as Mark Manson says in his book *The Subtle Art of Not Giving a F*ck,* we are in love with an idea about something, but hate the process of what it takes to get there, which means that we really aren't passionate about the thing itself, we're merely passionate about the idea of it. But, most often it's because we have developed a comfort zone for ourselves that we keep returning to over and over again, so if that something takes us out of our safe or easy zone, chances are we will clamor to return to it.

A comfort zone is what you're used to—a place within and without that is predictable, routine, and a feeling that is familiar. This doesn't necessarily mean that this place feels good or is even good for you. More often it's quite the opposite. Let's say that you come from a poor family and find yourself always struggling for money as an adult. You find that it's more comfortable to be broke because all of your friends are broke and that commonality is bonding. You are part of the tribe of your family and friends who share a lifestyle and a struggle. This group may take pot-shots at the wealthy and adhere to the tenets that life is hard, money is for the greedy, and wealth brings corruption. If I asked you if you want to be poor, I bet you would say, "Of course not!" And consciously you may believe that you are striving to becoming wealthier. However, subconsciously you are comfortable within the confines of what you've always known. If you were to become wealthy, how will the members of your tribe react? Would you lose them? Would you have to find a new way of relating and new people to get close to?

Let's call the people in your life your team. These are the people that have influenced, taught, inspired, assisted, pushed, and molded you and maybe even followed you.

You are as successful as the six people you spend the most time with. That goes for whom you choose to assist you, back you, emotionally support you, or inform you about what you wish to achieve. Whom you surround yourself with is important to your successes and failures. Is there an advantage to being surrounded by apathetic, uneducated, unmotivated, angry people? If you're the smartest one by a long shot then you may feel superior and your ego gets boosted, but ultimately your success will track the level at which you play, and ignorance can be a dangerous thing. This doesn't mean to turn your back on those you love, it simply means to look at your relationships—realign certain ones, distance from some, and spend more time with others.

We are tribal by nature and obtain a sense of belonging when we identify with some type of group. That group can be based on religion, sexual identity, politics, sports, a school or a club, or even our masculinity or femininity. Many groups implicitly (and sometimes overtly) ask us to dislike a particular "other" group of people as part of belonging. Brené Brown puts it best: "...asking members to dislike, disown, or distance themselves from another group of people as a condition of 'belonging' is always about control and power. I think we have to question the intentions of any group that insists on disdain toward other people as a membership requirement. It may be disguised as belonging, but real belonging doesn't necessitate disdain."

Any type of initial discomfort, especially when it involves discomfort with others, keeps us stuck in habits that we say we want to change or that need to change if we want to achieve certain things. Our fear of disconnection prevents us from taking healthier steps toward that change. These habits include emotional co-dependency, over-eating, workaholism, drinking, communication, withdrawal, and reinforcing a perspective.

Your perspective, the way you think and what you believe, is also part of your comfort zone. Some of those habits and beliefs work in your favor toward the vision you have for the life you want and others do not, but all feel comfortable, even the 'miserable' or 'frustrating' ones. If you look around you may notice people who continuously attract frustration into their lives. From an outside perspective, you can look at them and see that a minor change could eliminate that for them, yet they find excuses for not making that change over and over again and the frustration continues. Some accomplish a few things for a short time, some give it a great try but slide back to old habits, and few truly succeed in making sweeping change.

Isn't staying in a comfort zone a good thing? It can be a great thing in the moment in an area of your life that's rich and full. And it can be a good thing for a period of time for a number of reasons. However, if you remain in your same comfort zone for too long, then you can become stagnant and stop growing. Remember that if you're not growing you're dying. Our lives need a continuous stretch or they become rigid and immobile. And, considering that the world is constantly changing and evolving, we need to be too, so we can keep up. We need even more reach outside our comfort zones to make significant, lasting inner and outer changes in our lives.

If you want to know your past, look into your present conditions. If you want to know your future, look into your present actions. If you want to go from A, or the base of the mountain, to B, let's say to its peak, you must move. Sitting at A won't get you to B. Aside from often not knowing what we desire or not being fully committed to it, a major obstacle to getting our desires met is fear. Many people say it's failure, but Jack Lemmon said it nicely, "Failure seldom stops you. What stops you is the fear of failure." Most success stories are preceded by many failures along the way.

Fear is a larger, more deeply rooted and insidious feeling. No matter how much you think you are positioning yourself to attract a certain thing, if your underlying subconscious actions or intentions stem from fear, you are actually causing a blockage to that manifestation. Fear can be threaded through your intention or your actions in some way about which you are unaware. What are you afraid of? And how do you know?

Sometimes it takes action to lead back to your thoughts. It's like weeding—just when you think you got them all, you see another one. Knowing is becoming aware and awareness is not always instantaneous. Like becoming good at anything, it takes time. It's a process of assessing yourself and your willingness to be honest with yourself. The lies most of us tell, we first tell to ourselves, then we wonder why certain things aren't working out the way we say we wish they were. The key, of course, is really knowing what we desire and what lies we are telling ourselves. Most of us think we know what we want, but when we explore our desires honestly, we can be quite surprised to discover something different. The reason for this could be that we are calling in this other seemingly unwanted result through our reaction to a hidden fear.

One of the ways to uncover a fear is to look at your results and work backwards. If you say you want a committed loving relationship with a romantic partner, but consistently wind up with commitment-phobic individuals or partners who prove to be incompatible, then ask yourself why? Is it just because the available pool of what's out there is so bad or is it a message you're sending that you're unaware of? By exploring what message you may be sending, as an example, you may recognize that although your parents had a committed relationship they were miserable, so in your subconscious mind you fear a committed relationship because you equate it to misery. Thus you don't attract a committed relationship because, first and foremost, you believe it will be miserable. Once you have this awareness, you are able to make different decisions because you won't be ruled by a transparent, subconscious belief. What that means is that consciously, if someone were to ask you, "Do you believe committed relationships lead to misery?" you would absolutely and with certainty state that you do not believe that. However, when you peel away layers of what you cannot see, you discover that underneath it lies this very old belief from childhood that you can't imagine you hold—thus it is transparent to you, so hidden that you see through it without seeing that it's there at all—that indeed you have somehow equated commitment to misery. Now that you know you have the fear, the next step is being open and committed to change and to admit everything you see in yourself, to yourself.

The opposite of fear is love. They are two sides of the same coin. When you are fully in one, you are not in the other, yet you know both are there. When you find true joy in an activity, losing yourself completely to it, or being happy when around certain people, or feel a rush of excitement, those all stem from a place of love. When you make decisions stemming from love rather than fear, it shows in the results. As you would imagine, there are degrees of fear and love—a little fear with quite a bit of love, a lot of fear with a little love. Fear can be a necessary and healthy ingredient in certain situations and, of course, knowing when it works for us versus when it hinders us is the key. In any case, when a majority of your life decisions stem from love, this attitude attracts more of what you love into your life. Great love, like great success, involves great risk, which means first facing your fears. In order to face something, you must first be aware that you have it. Once you have the awareness, then you need to accept your fear. Only through acceptance can you then make a change. How do you make that change? By acting in spite of fear. That is the definition of courage. Once you find your courage, then you can ultimately break through to the other side of your fear.

Find what it is that you love and pursue that. Novelist W. Somerset Maugham wrote, "The greatest tragedy of life is not that men perish, but that they cease to love."

Your power lies in what you love, in what drives you, in where your passion lives. In *The Prophet*, Kahlil Gibran writes, "And think not you can direct the course of love, for love, if it finds you worthy, directs your course." Think about some of the extraordinary stories of people protecting their loved ones. The mother who lifts a car off of her child. A strength she couldn't possibly access without her fierce love driving it. What you love and what you value comes across to the world around you. It defines what you put your energy toward and energy is power. You've heard the saying "don't give away your power." Don't give away that which you hold sacred to you, that which is critically important and defines who you are. If you begin to give those pieces away you begin to lose your power.

Notice how when you have no interest in doing something but feel that you have to, how difficult it is to get motivated behind it. Some people procrastinate, some even get physically sick, some do it quickly and in haste, and others slog through. However, when you are interested and passionate about something, time flies and your attention seems boundless. There are things we all must do that we don't necessarily like doing or that are a "hassle"; however, when we put those things in the mix of the greater picture we are trying to achieve for ourselves and our lives, we can ascribe a different meaning to them and access our motivation. For example, let's say you are passionate about having your own business (your intention) selling art lights that you create (your desire). Part of that business is managing the money around the business, a task you dislike. However, that task is key to longevity and success, and with that understanding you learn and maintain that task so it becomes part of the mix of your power. Intention and desire have infinite organizing power.

Moving Into Action

When someone says *Just Do It*, you know exactly what they mean and those words can't help but spark a motivational reaction. Why are those three words so compelling that they have created an incredibly successful and worldwide brand? Human nature compels creation and to create a thing we must take action toward its creation. We are born curious, driven (if not for anything else, at the very least for survival), and desiring. We all seek something— love, money, comfort, beauty, health, whatever you can think of, with over seven billion people on this earth, someone is yearning for it. To get what you long for you must do something toward that end, even if all you do is say that you desire it. For most of us it's not that easy or simple. Getting what we seek takes numerous steps beginning first with knowing what that *it* is, figuring out what it takes to get it, then taking the actions necessary to reach that goal.

Even if we fail, there is satisfaction in knowing that we tried. Many reports have shown that the majority of people, before they die, say that any regrets they have exist around that which they didn't do or try to do, that which they never even made an attempt to attain but secretly wished for. If there is a secret yearning in you, don't bury it. Explore what it would require for you to give it a shot and take the steps toward achieving it.

There are people too busy with the basics of survival to strive for much more. We are fortunate that even if we are in survival mode, we live in a society where some opportunity is within reach. It may require one tiny reach at a time, but step after step can lead to a bigger opportunity that you could never have had without the first steps. Focusing on surviving from day-to-day doesn't leave much time to motivate you to do more; however, if you let apathy set it in, you certainly can't move beyond a stagnant circumstance. This is where your inner life, your yearning, your understanding of self, your vision for yourself is a vital component to your best life. Every day, find something or someone that inspires you and begin with one inspirational thought or vision for yourself, then begin to add to that with more and more thoughts day-by-day and, over time, see if a slow shift doesn't begin to occur.

Apathy and boredom come from stagnation. If you are bored, it's because you are not compelled to do or think anything. If you are unmotivated, get moving and chances are you can shift and open a portal toward motivation and connection. You won't and can't get anywhere if you are standing still. If you are not growing, you are dying; growth is motion. *Just do it* is an internal call to yourself.

Sometimes getting what you desire would mean huge changes in your life. If you are not prepared or ready to accept that, you may never get what it is you wish for because your overriding fear of change will prevent it.

Action is the bridge between your inner world and the outer world and opportunities present themselves inviting you to bridge that gap. An opportunity is a set of circumstances that makes it possible to do something. The marks of a good opportunity are ones that give you a way to show off your talents, to show what you can do, or to emphasize who you are. Successful people are constantly learning and growing and are initially inclined to approach opportunities with an open mind toward a yes attitude so as to see all of its value. They seize the possibilities and examine them to see if they can work in their favor.

Not all opportunities lead you to a pot of gold, but they do contribute to your experience and knowledge base. You may have to kiss many frogs along the way. There is nothing so valuable as experience and you cannot have experiences without taking chances.

Once you make a decision to pursue a particular set of circumstances, go with it. Don't keep second-guessing yourself because that will keep you stalled—your mental momentum will stop and you will have to start over—and it could prevent you from succeeding. The moment of absolute certainty rarely appears. Even if your decision doesn't bring the results you desired, don't dwell in regret. Take from it what worked, what didn't, and any information that can assist you in the future. You never know why a situation presented itself to you. Sometimes you need to go through a bad situation so that you don't keep attracting them and can move on to good ones. Know that it will lead you to what you need to experience next.

Fight Or Flight?

Do you think that changing where you live, your associates, your job, your home, your city or even your country will alone change the fundamentals of your life? For a time they may. If the change you make comes from a place of taking action toward the fulfillment of a dream, then it's the correct change; but if it comes from a place of dissatisfaction with current circumstances and simply a way to escape where you are right now, then the change won't be a real solution.

One of the reasons some people don't get what they seek is that they don't know why they seek it. What is motivating you to want a specific thing or the change you're chasing after? What is the emotion driving you to go after this change? If it's simply not wanting to deal with the circumstances in which you find yourself and thinking that starting over in some way will make it all go away, then you are running—taking flight. When you flee in this manner, what you will discover is that in your new circumstances suddenly the same issues begin to crop up, the same problems begin to form, and the same dissatisfaction sets in. Why? Because **wherever you go you take yourself with you.**

We're all familiar with the notion of fight or flight as a survival mechanism. I'd like to consider an alternative way to use 'fight' in this instance. The notion of not fleeing, and instead 'fighting', means that you first stay put and really look to see what the root problem is. What is really blocking the fulfillment you seek? Chances are there is a core fear that you bring to every place and situation, which, until you deal with it, will control the results of your life. The first step in the "fight" is to uncover your root fear, that inner setting that prevents you from soaring toward your desires. As an example, let's say that you discover that you fear being the "bad guy" in a situation so you don't want to rock the boat and have your family and friends see you as selfish or greedy. As you know, our fears are merely false expectations appearing real, so you won't know for sure what other's reactions will be; but now that you see that this is your fear, ask yourself, "What if they think I'm the bad guy just because I now have what I really desire and am happy and successful? Are they good guys to want me not to be happy?" Once you are willing to accept whatever others think of you, then you can take a step toward making a change. Now that first step or action begins the cycle for everything to change because the motion part of Newton's Law (a body in motion will tend to remain in motion and a body at rest will tend to remain at rest) is engaged and you are on your way—you now have the power and the energy of momentum on your side. Hopefully, this ends the urge to flee for flight's sake.

To help you think about your motivations, I'd like to give you a couple of examples from characters in film. In the classic *The Graduate*, at the beginning of the film Ben graduates from college and is confused and paralyzed about his future. Then Mrs. Robinson offers herself to him and, although he resists at first, he eventually succumbs and his motivation is revealed when he tells her he's doing it out of boredom. He chooses to focus on the affair rather than on his real problem. He then gets together with Elaine, Mrs. Robinson's daughter, and after only one date decides he wants to continue seeing her despite her mother's warnings to stay away. That becomes his quest to the exclusion of all else. The question then becomes: does Ben pursue Elaine because he's really in love with her or as a way to immerse himself in a "project" or challenge because he still can't face the real problem of the next steps for his future? If it's really love, then he's fought the good fight; but if it's the latter, then it's flight. The last scene, where Ben and Elaine sit next to each other on a bus, after Ben took her from the altar where she was about to marry another man, reminds us that the original problem still remains, and now with additional complications.

In *The Runaway Bride*, every time Maggie finds herself at the altar, she runs. Why? Her root problem is that she hasn't allowed herself to know who she really is, what she likes and seeks and strives for, and to fully be herself. As way of avoiding herself, she takes on the likes and dislikes of the men in her life and for a moment thinks she can mold herself into their lives and continue to avoid herself. However, she has enough of a nagging in the back of her mind not to go through with the marriages at the last minute because none of the men are really a match, until she meets Ike and resolves to look inward.

If you know you want some change but don't know where to begin, ask yourself, "Who do I aspire to be as a person?" Not a career, not the amount of money you want to have, not the size of house or car or awards. Rather, the person that is left after all of that is stripped away, that which remains with others when you are gone. The mark left on the hearts of others is the whom of who you are. Use this personal aspiration to help you define what you want. Then take those definitions of the person you want to be and use it to go after that which you desire to create.

If you don't feel motivated, waiting for motivation to arrive before you take any action isn't the recipe for achievement. It's the other way around—start doing and notice your motivation rising. It's easy to lose sight of the fact that you won't always feel like doing something, but that you need to do it anyway if you want to achieve something or to remain true to whom you say you want to be.

Dealing With Obstacles

How you approach your problems sets up their outcome and effect on you. If you are like most people, you will do almost anything to avoid problems or complications. If you see a challenge with several obviously difficult obstacles, do you turn and go elsewhere or do you think about finding your way through? If you turn away and are pursuing the same goal, you will discover that another challenge arises and the cycle begins all over again. All great achievements, successes, and fulfilling endeavors are filled with challenges and require overcoming obstacles. For those who complain that they aren't successful or fulfilling their dreams or doing what they want or living where they want, the irony is that in their quest to avoid problems they have created the biggest problem of all: dissatisfaction and very possibly more problems of an entirely different nature. The secret is not to avoid or cower away from obstacles; it's to grow yourself so that you are bigger than any problem you face, to contend with it and to get to the other side.

How do you grow yourself? I would ask you to begin with working on yourself and your perspective, your courage, your confidence, and your abilities. When you approach a problem seeing it as overwhelming, then you will be overwhelmed and buried under its weight. Stop focusing on the size of your problems and begin focusing on the size of yourself and who you are capable of being.

Problems give rise to creativity, which is your opportunity to create solutions. There is a difference between challenges and obstacles. Challenges are problems that test and tax you. To meet them you are being asked to stretch yourself, to try your skills above what you are used to. In other words, the implication is that you are being asked to better yourself. Obstacles are defined as barriers, deterrents, or obstructions in addition to problems or complications and can be psychologically debilitating. Yet, if you learn to look at obstacles in much the same way as challenges, then the word obstacle will lose its charge and can be approached in much the same way as a challenge.

In the documentary film *Man On A Wire*, Philippe Petit, the subject of the film, had both a huge challenge and obstacles. The challenge was to walk on a wire between the two World Trade Center towers, the highest buildings in the world still under final construction at the time. The obstacle was that access was prohibited at the top, and this type of act was not only forbidden, but highly illegal and dangerous. For years, he prepared for the challenge and for months he garnered a team and a plan to get him over the obstacles. Each member of his team was critical to his success and to this unparalleled achievement in history. In 1974, he gracefully made his way between the towers without any physical supports or net. His vision was so great and certain that he couldn't imagine not doing it.

Do you complain about how people throw their trash onto the street, yet every time you walk by a piece of trash on the ground you don't pick it up and put it in the trash bin that may be just feet away? We've become experts at blaming others for their shortcomings and their "bad" behavior, yet when it comes to rolling up our sleeves and taking a step to clean up something for the greater good, we don't consider it our responsibility because we didn't create it. It's much the same with how we see obstacles to our goals. We complain about them because in our mind we say, "I didn't create that so why should I be the one to take care of it and have everyone else benefit?" But many times our actions toward eliminating a particular obstacle or two can be of great benefit to ourselves as well. And what's wrong with benefiting our community along the way?

Kindness costs you nothing yet its rewards are vast. Practicing kindness in the face of obstacles hones your skills as a master of your universe. There's a tale about a boulder that a king put in the middle of the road, which made passage incredibly inconvenient and for some quite difficult. The king wanted to see if anyone would remove the huge obstacle. Most of his subjects, including his own courtiers and wealthiest merchants, simply took the long way, walking around it, having their subordinates maneuver heavy loads through more treacherous grounds and complained how the king wasn't keeping the roads clear. No one bothered to do anything about clearing the road themselves. Then a peasant came along with a load of wheat and, when he came upon the boulder, he stopped, put his load down and tried several ways to get the boulder off the road. After many attempts, he finally figured out a solution and moved the rock to the side of the road, clearing the passage. Returning to his wheat, he noticed that something had been left under the boulder. A bag lay in the middle of the road. Inside were many gold coins and a note from the king indicating that the gold was for the person who removed the boulder from the road. Every obstacle presents an opportunity. You can complain or you can do something about it.

Self-obsession appears to have reached new heights with selfies, constant photo taking of each other and ourselves, and instant self-promotion tools at our disposal. The way we look has become a growing obsession. According to the National Society of Plastic Surgeons, total minimally invasive cosmetic procedures (including things like Botox and fillers) have risen 168 percent from 2000 to 2018. More than 50 percent of the plastic surgeons say that they have many patients who want the procedure in order to look better in selfies. One could argue that this exhibits another kind of void.

Constantly examining the way you look and working to make your face or body more 'perfect' keeps you focused on what you see as 'wrong' and that something needs constant 'fixing.' This can create great anxiety and one injection of Botox may relieve that anxiety, but only for a moment, until you see the next imperfection. When you are simply focused on how you appear, you may forget some of the more critical elements necessary to creating your happiness and success and that of the society/community in which you live and are a part. When you are young then celebrity and the number of likes you get to your photos on Instagram may seem like something tangible and worth striving for. However, as you age, the notion of looking 'perfect' not only becomes more of a full-time job, and you discover, much like Orlando, the character in Virginia Wolf's book, that in the end he wasn't looking for fame, wealth, or honors as much as he simply wanted true companionship. Small aesthetic imperfections are not genuine obstacles and can consume much of your time without giving you real results.

When you recognize that your actions as well as your non-actions have a larger effect, you may choose to make different choices along the way. There are no obstacles—only opportunities to choose again. Journalist Michael Pollan reminds us that "...that's the challenge—to change the system more than it changes you."

Reflections:

1. Think of something you've attempted to achieve, but did not. Why do you think you didn't? Do you care that you didn't achieve it? If you do care, did you try again? Would you? If so, what would you do differently?

2. Is there anything you know you need to do or want to do to achieve a potential benefit for yourself (a phone call or a trip you need to make, a contact you need to find, an audition to sign up for, a job to pursue), but it's too uncomfortable, so you don't? What would happen if you did it anyway?

3. List some things that you consider to be obstacles to one of your goals. If you looked at the things on your list differently, could you see how some may actually be turned into opportunities?

4. Name one person, decision, or experience you've been avoiding. Why? Examine your answer and dig deeper.

Chapter Nine

WHAT IMPACT DO YOU HAVE?

We all have an impact on our world—probably much bigger than we realize. If you think that you live a small, insignificant life because you're not famous, or don't have tens of thousands of Instagram followers, or aren't on television or being written about, I would like you to think again. The coronavirus began with one individual and spread to the entire world. It is our media culture and technology that is a large player in why we may feel so inadequate or ineffectual. The reality is quite different. Know that each choice you make, no matter how small—from what you eat, what you buy, how you live, where you put your trash, what you say, how you say it, to whom you say it, if you smile, if you snarl, if you run, if you act, if you withdraw, if you lie, if you are honest, if you forgive, if you harbor anger, if you extend love—has an impact in directing us as a whole. If a butterfly flapping its wings in Brazil affects the wind currents at the North Pole, imagine what impact each of our seemingly "insignificant" actions have.

No man is an island. We are social beings. Some are more so than others, but we are a species dependent on one another. When there is strife in a region or great inequities, there is a collective anxiety that affects everyone. In their book *The Inner Level: How More Equal Societies Reduce Stress, Restore Sanity and Improve Everyone's Well Being*, Richard Wilkinson and Kate Pickett make some valid points. One of them is that anxiety contributes to a variety of mental-health problems, including depression, narcissism, and schizophrenia, which are growing at alarming rates in the United States. They point out that group interaction and cooperation have been an essential component of humanity's evolutionary success. They also make a case for vast inequality in a society affecting even the wealthy in detrimental ways. The Centers for Disease Control and Prevention (CDC), reported that 47,000 Americans took their own lives in 2017. The CDC data showed that the national suicide rate has increased 33 percent between 1999 and 2017 and has increased every year since. Americans kill themselves at a higher rate than those in other advanced countries. The United States is the world's richest country, yet wealthy people such as Kate Spade and Anthony Bourdain have not been immune. Ever since Emile Durkheim's seminal 1987 book *Suicide*, suicide has been considered a disturbing indicator of underlying social problems. According to the data, America's social problems are growing more dire.

We no longer have the luxury of arguing the moral validity of any particular war. The destructive capacity of our world is so enormous that it overwhelms the combined destructive capacity of humankind throughout time. To deny the truth that war is destructive is absurd. We can no longer sit in our comfortable living rooms and say the rest of the world be damned. We are all participants in the world and what one does affects us all. There is nothing clever or smart about doing whatever we want without a care about its effects on others. When another suffers, so do you, most of us just aren't consciously aware of it unless it's someone very close; but the ripple affect of our actions, however imperceptible, is there.

Do you ever think that a particular person has too much power, and that your vote, or your small action, or your little self can't make any difference? In some situations, if you're looking for an immediate outcome or result, that is true. However, if you learn to look at the big picture, you will see that every seemingly inconsequential action adds up with every other action and begins to amount to something real and tangible. The more focused you are and the more steps you take within your circle of influence, the larger your circle and your influence becomes.

While you alone may not be able to sway an election, you can and do have an impact on those around you and in your world. If you are a passive person who doesn't get involved, you give those around you more power and say over events in your world. However, every action you take and every statement you make or don't make does have an effect, whether you realize it or not. For example: you're an executive professional woman at a dinner party and one of the guests, a wealthy man, makes a statement that women belong in the home because the men are the ones that should do the "important" work and you just smile politely as others laugh and indulge him. In that moment, you are complicit in his comment. By your silence, you are essentially endorsing his statement and shrinking yourself within the context of the group. If the situation is sensitive and an outright challenge could create problems, then you are at least obligated to pose a question or a reciprocal joke to put another side forth, such as "I'm sure Angela Merkel, the Chancellor of Germany, would appreciate that." If you do not stand up for what you know to be wrong, you become part of the problem and hinder the change you say you want to see.

We seem to have lost sight of the fact that it is okay to disagree. We can disagree and still remain colleagues, even friends. We are human. We come from different backgrounds, have different beliefs and perspectives. Disagreement is good for promoting thinking. It is a way for us to work out our own ideas, or to strengthen our viewpoint, or to perhaps even change or expand our viewpoint. True challenging discourse can lead to seeing something new, expanding our knowledge, or illuminating areas where we may have been ignorant. View disagreement as an opportunity to learn something new. Don't view it as a way to turn your back on someone or as an opportunity to shame. Use disagreement as an opportunity to open conversation and allow for discourse where thinking and challenging is a channel to greater understanding.

If you are a vocal and active person, you sometimes can see the results of your actions right away, but more often than not they only add up over time and can feel imperceptible. But, there comes a time when you reach a tipping point and suddenly that change is visible and real.

In his book *7 Habits of Highly Successful People*, Stephen Covey talks about how within the entire universe of our concerns, there are some things we can influence and some things we can only stay concerned about.

Many people choose to focus much of their attention on the

things that are outside of their circle of influence. Things that they can individually do nothing about, such as the shortcomings of other people, global capitalism, the weather, a troubled childhood, or bad luck. These are the things they focus on and complain about without any ability for remedial action on their part. That's not to say you shouldn't have discussions on these topics or learn about them. Those are positive actions. What's not positive is merely complaining based on what you hear. If you are so focused, then this focus leads to a cycle of more and more blaming and accusing and to feelings of victimization. This prevents you from taking any positive action toward any kind of change. Focusing on the negatives without a potential for positive discussion puts more negativity out into the world, which perpetuates that which you are complaining about in the first place. Your negative way of thinking, along with failing to take steps to change things, results in your circle of influence shrinking.

Your essence is tested in the most desperate and challenging of circumstances. It is during those times that you truly discover who you are and can decide who you want to be. Your past cannot be undone, but your present and future are yours to mold.

Influence does not mean control. Your daily behavior, your actions, your inactions, and your words are continuously influencing the world around you. By proactively and consciously focusing on the things you wish to change, on that which matters to you, on being and standing for that which you believe in, your influence grows. Your actions, your words, who you are, and how you present yourself are the essence of manifestation.

It's not about immediate gratification, it's about who you are that will determine your legacy, your influence on the world around you and on the generations to come.

Leadership and Your Influence

Who do you consider a leader? I don't believe that giving someone a title and putting them into a position over others automatically bestows leadership. Leadership is a quality that comes from first being the kind of person others want to follow. True leaders stand the test of time. They have taken and take risks in their life. They try new things, they innovate, they think for themselves and, above all, they are accountable.

There are those who are charismatic and talented at spin and salesmanship, who can gather people to support them or to do their bidding for a short while, much like a snake-oil salesman, but they are not true, lasting leaders. I heard an insightful program on NPR about the dangerously charismatic leaders in our history, such as Hitler and Mussolini, and what happens to people in a live crowd when they are in the presence of such individuals. The research shows that a majority of people become awestruck by these charismatic people to the point that it overrides their common sense and allows them to completely ignore facts that would benefit their own good and survival. These charismatic people are not true leaders, but are instead master manipulators and, frequently, bullies.

Real leadership is earned just as trust is earned and those who would follow you must first trust you. Leadership is influence and by nature relational. Truly great leaders who have earned the right to lead are not in leadership solely for personal gain and saving everything for themselves. They lead in order to serve others, and they perform to the highest level of which they are capable. The leaders whose inspiration and influence lives on are the men and women who helped people live better lives and to reach their potential, such as Martin Luther King, Jr., Nelson Mandela, Ruth Bader Ginsberg, and Mahatma Gandhi. That is the highest calling of leadership: to share your knowledge and power and to empower others.

Language is important. Let's say you are in a situation where you are in a position of some type of leadership, such as the role of a boss, and you're not getting what you want from your team, or you see something detrimental occurring that could ultimately be bad for your bottom line or your productivity. If you speak of what is not happening rather than what is happening, you will not get to a solution quickly, rather you will stay mired in complaint because your focus is on what's not happening. Trying to motivate others when you make them feel shame or failure is difficult. Instead, speak directly of what is happening and what change is needed. This leads to accountability—you are taking ownership and allowing others to take ownership. You are pointing out that, collectively, we have this problem and here's where we are without creating blame on how we got there. With that approach, the door opens for you speak about what you want to happen, how the problem can be solved, and what actions need to follow for a successful resolution.

We are all leaders on some level in some area of our life. If you're a parent, you are the leader in your children's lives. There are hierarchies and opportunities for leadership everywhere—the workplace, your social circle, your family, an online venue, a club you belong to. Leadership is not in the number of followers, rather the quality of your message and its positive effects on even one other person. The mark of a great leader is one who inspires even just one other great leader.

This brings me to the current state of our nation's leadership. Democracy is not a spectator sport. Without individual involvement, we, as a nation, couldn't have had the civil-rights movement, change in leadership after Watergate, the end of war in Vietnam, women's right to vote, and other changes that affect the way we live. Are your freedoms important to you? Do you want to feel safe? Do you want to be able to speak freely without being shot? Do you want to know that if you are violated, justice will be sought on your behalf? Do you want to be able to love whom you choose without retribution? I hear people shout "I have rights!" when backed into a corner or when trying to prove a point, but those same people don't vote or get engaged in acting on issues they believe in. What if you didn't have all the rights you feel entitled to and take for granted? There are many, in fact most, places on earth that don't have such rights.

People from so many other countries dream of coming to the United States. Why? Freedom. For those of us who've never known anything but this freedom, we tend to take if for granted and disregard that that freedom can be taken away, even if only bit by bit. Over time, we tend to get used to everything and begin taking things for granted. Then an incident such as the murder of George Floyd occurs and becomes an undeniable and broadly public event and we are finally forced to address the inequities of our system.

If you want or expect society to work in your favor, you must be an active participant in it. Many of us believe that no matter what we do the larger public systems of justice, health care, infrastructure, and eduction will stay the same and our lives will be basically the same. For a time, that was probably more true than not. However, times keep changing and we can see that certain rights have come perilously close to being obliterated in the U.S. We came close to losing the woman's right to choose, and in the last several years, we have already severely dismantled reproductive rights. We've already and imperceptibly lost part of our right to privacy with Homeland Security using its powers indiscriminately to listen to and read our private communications. Our prisons are overcrowded with minor offenders creating more criminals rather than rehabilitating them. With changes in Texas allowing re-writing of historical textbooks for kids to incorporate faith rather than fact, the impact can last for generations. The response to COVID-19 has upended and ended lives. Don't think that these changes won't have huge impacts on us all.

Do you have any obligation to the community and to the world you live in? The answer to that question can go either way. If you expect certain liberties such as a justice system with checks and balances to avert senseless brutality from authority; the opportunity to get good and immediate medical help; an advanced infrastructure upon which to travel; functioning, affordable utilities; a certain amount of safety and protection from crime and violation, then the answer is yes. If you don't care about these things, and will not complain about them, then the answer is no, because forfeiting your participation also forfeits your right to whine and complain.

Do you have any responsibility to participate? The next time you are asked to support someone running for a position of any kind, think about what that means and what your support says about you. If you support someone only because you think others in your group think it's the thing to do, but you really don't know what that person stands for, then you are being passive yet still affecting an outcome. When you are passive, you are making a statement and inadvertently participating. What would our world look like if we were all passive? Others can control you or secure your vote only if you let them. Inquire within about everything and seek your own information and verification.

There are many things happening in the world and the results depend on how they are handled by our leaders and in turn by every one of us. Democracy starts with each one of us. What we do affects our community. When we affect our community, then we can branch out and have a greater impact. Change begins with one, then another and then another. Sitting back and complaining does not create results. Sitting idly by doesn't change anything.

It is in your interest to become informed, to know who controls the little things, the small rules in your life, in your neighborhood, your schools, your streets, your police, your city. Sometimes it may be inconvenient, or you may be exhausted, but if you want a voice, you must speak up and you must vote. Without voting, you have no voice.

Do some due diligence on your own and know whom you are voting for. Ask what that person has done in their life, how and what have they voted for in the past, what policies do they really support and what they are against. In what ways is that person like you, how are they different in what they value, and how will their background and experience affect issues in your life? How experienced and/or educated are they? Experience and education is a plus for anyone in a leadership role. We want our leaders to be the best of us, not the most average or lesser.

And, in the case of ballot measures, know what you are voting for. This can sometimes be tricky because each side attempts to spin the information on the measure to get you to vote their way and that can mean omitting or inflating certain facts. Investigate what that measure really means in a practical way to your life, what affects it can have on you and your community, and where the common sense behind the vote lies. Why is it on the ballot? This may sound like a pain, but with the Internet at your fingertips it wouldn't take much of your time and could make a huge difference to our collective future, one person at a time. The generations that came before us fought hard for our freedoms, let's not let it be for nothing. You are accountable for the choices you make in whom you vote for and if you don't vote.

You are also accountable for the information you disseminate. We've been subjected to an overwhelming amount of fake news. Part of the reason is that we pass it on without considering the source or more subtle pieces of information that would tip us off that it may not be real. Whether in business, politics, community, or personal matters, where your information comes from is important to how you consider it. The first question to examine is who do you listen to and why?

You may hear people say the phrase "It's not personal it's just business"; however, how you handle a situation, how you behave, what you say, are all a reflection of who you are and are quite personal regardless of the area of life. When was getting fired "just business" to the one getting chopped? The phrase is often used when delivering unfortunate news or backing out of an agreement or terminating a contract. Bad outcomes do and will happen and they are a part of life, but the statement that it's not personal is merely a way to deflect the humanity of the situation. Sometimes the phrase is also used to take away any moral or ethical responsibility from a situation and to sanitize it. If it affects people's jobs, their quality of life, their time, their responsibilities, expectations...of course it is personal. There are times the phrase is used in place of a real explanation of the truth, which is a cowardly move. If you are tempted to use the phrase, ask yourself what it is you're really trying to avoid saying.

When looking at situations regarding politics or business, some questions to consider are: Is your information coming from an expert source that has a proven track record? Is the information accurate and provable or merely conjecture? Does your source have a separate agenda? What is their primary agenda? How is the messaging delivered? Is the information in service to your best interests? Is the information being effectively and honestly delivered?

When it comes to more personal situations, assess the people you listen to and those that affect you. Look at their lives and who they are as people. What is your relationship or agreement with them? Do you respect them? Do you admire them for any particular reason? Are they kind, fair, and reasonable? Are they honest? Do they have an agenda? Are they able to put their own interests aside when assessing a situation?

Some hard realities are that, first, not everyone likes or will like you; second, you can't please everyone; and third, people lie. The fact that people lie, for an inordinate amount of reasons, is exactly why facts, rather than opinions, are critical. Before you allow others to readily ruin your day, consider the why of a situation and the source from where it originates. Are they reacting to something in their own lives and taking it out on you? Are they jealous for some reason? Are they upset at themselves and wanting you to fix it? There could be a million scenarios. First, consider the source. Second, if the source is worthy, then consider the information and the facts that may or may not support it. Third, consider how the information affects you and if and how you can use it for your or others' benefit. Above all else, be true to the highest and best vision of yourself and act accordingly.

> *"You are what your deep, driving desire is. As your desire is, so is your will. As your will is, so is your deed. As your deed is, so is your destiny."*
>
> Brihadaranyaka Upanishad IV.4.5

When we are born into this world, our essential nature is one of pure potentiality. It is from there that we begin our indoctrination into the world as it is presented to us by others and then limits begin to be imposed. Knowing yourself is the key to tapping into that pure potential. We experience the world in two ways: self-referral and object-referral. In self-referral, our internal reference point is ourselves, our intuition, our own unique internal perspective unfettered by others. In object-referral, we are influenced by everything outside of ourselves, by other people, objects, circumstances, and by situations, and we are seeking the approval of others and have a need to control things in our life.

When operating from self-referral there is an absence of fear because you are not seeking approval or control or validation from anything or anyone outside yourself. This is a place where you are tapped into yourself and the pure potential that you came into the world with. It's a place where you put aside all of the limits and obstacles and fears you have learned and created in your life. This is the place of possibility.

Object-referral is based on fear and the ego. Here is where obstacles continue and are readily created. The power you create through object-referral is always tenuous and dependent on others, while the power you create from self-referral is permanent. To learn more on accessing your ability for self-referral read *The Seven Spiritual Laws of Success* by Deepak Chopra. A good way to tap into your self-referral is through meditation.

To meditate is defined as thinking deeply or focusing your mind for a period of time, in silence or with the aid of chanting. It is defined as thinking, but it is not thinking in the way we typically use the word, where we break down facts and assess pros and cons and think about the things and people around us in relationship to us or other things. There is much confusion about meditation because of this fairly inaccurate definition. The purpose of meditation is to silence the mind's chatter, to feel the center of yourself, to tap into that vast potential, and to allow yourself to fall into it. To meditate is to go within. It is a place of self-referral. In meditation the mind is clear, relaxed and inwardly focused. You are fully awake and alert when you meditate, but your mind is not focused on the external world or on the events taking place around you. The practice of meditation requires an inner state that is still and one-pointed, or focused, so that the mind becomes silent. When the mind is silent and no longer distracts you, you fall into a deeper state of meditation and experience freedom from your mind chatter, which allows you to access inner joy, contentment, relief, and inner relaxation. This is the place you connect with your true self.

Allow yourself to do your own thing. With the fast-paced changes happening in the world, people's desires and needs are shifting, our resources are shifting, and social changes are happening on a global scale. How do you feel about your world? What moves you? What upsets you? What do you feel, on a deeper level, is right and/or wrong for you? There are new opportunities for doing things and new industries that are sprouting. Allow yourself to explore beyond your comfort zone, beyond what are you are told, beyond what you see others doing, and set your imagination free with new possibility.

Novelist Franz Kafka wrote, "You need not leave your room. Remain sitting at your table and listen. You need not even listen, simply wait. You need not even wait, just learn to become quiet, and still, and solitary. The world will freely offer itself to you to be unmasked. It has no choice; it will roll in ecstasy at your feet."

Reflections:

1. *Who has regularly in the past or currently come to you for advice? Why do you think that is?*

2. *Is there anyone in your life who emulates how you vote, what you do, what you wear, or some of the other choices you make? If you have*

children, think about the ways you in which you are their role model. Think about the things you tell them are right or wrong? What impact did your parents have on you? What impact do you think you will have on your own children?

3. Who do you look up to in your life? Why?

4. How do you participate in your community or your workplace? Why do you do it?

Chapter Ten

WHERE DO YOU GO FROM HERE?

I invite you to strive to be a person of great character. If you believe that you cannot or that it is too late for you, then your journey ends here, because what you believe is what you experience. I believe it is never too late, and anyone can grow and better themselves. I invite you to choose yourself as a person of character. If you begin and take the first steps toward that goal and continue to take step by step, then one day you may wake up and realize that that is exactly what you have become.

Keep learning. Knowledge is power and it will keep you growing. No matter how old you are, learning is a key component to a vibrant, successful life. Learning is a life-long endeavor if you want to stay younger, flourish, feel more energetic, and progress. Does this mean taking formal classes? For some of you it might, but for most of us it may mean exploring other cultures, training in a particular field, reading and researching or experiencing new aspects of life, and it can be done in hundreds of different ways.

When you are in the company of people who are knowledgable, conversation is more interesting, the opportunity to expand your own ideas and your business or job increases, there's a stronger tendency to engage in life, to create, to innovate. Be proud of your knowledge. Don't shrink to fit a social situation. Many young women dumb down their level of intelligence so as not to intimidate a date or to be better liked by a group of girlfriends. Some men do the same, for example, not to outdo their bosses. This is a dis-service to all. Help raise others up rather than step down to their level. One of the most brilliant and inspiring quotes is attributed to Nelson Mandela; however, in reality it comes from the book *A Return to Love* by Marianne Williamson: "...Our deepest fear is not that we are inadequate. Our deepest fear is that we are powerful beyond measure. It is our light, not our darkness that most frightens us. We ask ourselves, Who am I to be brilliant, gorgeous, talented, fabulous? Actually, who are you not to be? You are a child of God. Your playing small does not serve the world. There is nothing enlightened about shrinking so that other people won't feel insecure around you. We are all meant to shine, as children do. We were born to make manifest the glory of God that is within us. It's not just in some of us; it's in everyone. And as we let our own light shine, we unconsciously give other people permission to do the same. As we are liberated from our own fear, our presence automatically liberates others."

When people are afraid to speak their minds, then those who are the biggest bullies win with their ideas and their agenda. The few people who are willing to step up and to speak up are the ones who are truly maintaining our democracy and are the ones who, throughout history, make a big difference. I'm not talking about those individuals who claim to speak up, but in reality only spin and propagate an agenda for personal or corporate benefit that has no basis in fact or a sound knowledge base behind it. This is another reason to stay educated—so that you can tell the difference between those who are merely trying to persuade you to their way of thought to fulfill an agenda versus those who are teaching you something based on their actual experience and for your benefit and imparting actual concepts based in fact or facts themselves. The greatest people in history took their knowledge, their understanding, and spoke their mind, and they continued to learn, to take in their experiences, and they made adjustments as necessary. They weren't afraid to stand up for what they believed in, because they had the knowledge (facts, information, evidence, and in some cases intuitive knowledge) to back up their beliefs. They also weren't afraid to change course if circumstances or information came to light requiring that change. The more you know, the better choices you can make.

Before you judge another, take the time to explore what it must be like to walk in their shoes. That's part of gathering information and continuing your education. Know when to speak up and when to take in and observe. But don't fool yourself into thinking that when you're silent out of fear and cowardice that you're observing because speaking up isn't appropriate. It's easier to speak up, to have conviction, when you have the expertise to support you. Know what you're talking about, make sure you have as much information you can get your hands on, do your due diligence, and don't be afraid to be flexible or to be wrong in light of new information. There is nothing shameful about being wrong. Throughout your life, there is always something to learn. No one is ever finished learning unless they decide to stop growing and begin dying.

While you are exploring ways in which to increase your knowledge base, begin with the things you are involved in already. If you work for or own a company, think about and gather information that will serve not only the company and yourself but the humanity you are an inextricable part of. Executives are asked (and for many, their bonuses depend on it) to at least sustain, and more often to increase, already high profits every year. Is this responsible? In order to keep increasing profits that will be distributed to shareholders and executives rather than consistently putting some of that money back into creating a better business for society and for the people working in it, something will have to give over time. There's an ugly end game here where, in order to achieve those profits, the company short-shrifts the product by using cheaper materials that will ensure breakage and a need for consumers to re-purchase part or all on a shorter cycle, or they begin to exclude quality checks or safety that can impact their workforce. Can we sustain ever-growing profits and still create environments that are healthful to the local economies, to pay people living wages, to educate them, and to not to harm the environment and our own bodies? What if a five to fifteen percent annual profit was considered more than enough for the shareholders and the extra money beyond that went back into the company and the community? Companies should be and need to be profitable, but I believe that this should not be accomplished at the expense of life. What are your thoughts on this and the work that you do?

Any change must begin with each individual. Many of us have become disconnected with the reality of what is happening all around us and the leaders of large corporations in general and their investors have become so insulated from what's really going on in their own businesses and the world around them that it's time to begin the dialogue. Think about the stock you may own, the way you do business, who you work with and for. Where are you putting your money, your energy, your support? Begin the discussion, raise the questions, explore the answers, and think about it.

You have this one life and during this fleeting time you have the ability to be and accomplish anything you want, provided you use your time wisely. Spend your time on the things that are most important to you. On those things that you most value.

Do you wish to have a positive impact? One that betters this world and the lives in it? Or are you just out for yourself and making sure that your life is meeting your material needs? I would like to suggest that if you create a life that truly meets your inner needs, you will likely have a positive impact, at least on those around you. Those inner needs would include love, healthy relationships, and respect for life and your surroundings.

We all have an affect on each other and no one is immune. If you are an executive or owner of a chemical or other pharmaceutical company, ask yourself what your goals are besides earning a profit. Are your chemicals harmful to living things? Under all or just certain circumstances? To the environment? Addictive? Unhealthful? Lead to other much greater problems rather than solutions? If the answer to any of those questions is a yes and you then try to come up with excuses for why it's okay, then please do some more digging in your soul. If you are part of a team peddling a product that creates unnecessary excess in some way or is merely an impulsive throw away, ask yourself these questions: Is the byproduct of this more harmful or helpful to humanity?

I see many wasteful products being created, such as plastic toys used as promotional incentives that little kids would scream to get, then throw away the next day. I see reams and reams of nothing but over-packaged goods of items no one used or needed for more than a passing moment in their lives. Yet those products are part of the Pacific floating island of trash spanning more than 600,000 square miles (twice the size of Texas!) and growing every day. And it's not the only one out there. I think the reason this is not a positive thing is obvious.

I see many people living in a bubble, unwilling to look at some painful facts. They tune in only to those they want to hear. Denial is a chosen ignorance. I believe that our world can no longer afford ignorance. Self-awareness is where each of us can begin. People respect and trust those whom they consider they can rely on and are honest. Know what you can and cannot deliver to those around you. Speak your truth. Stand up for what you believe in. Speak up and support those you love and admire. You are unique—embrace it.

We each have an obligation to do what we can toward sustaining a fulfilling future. Self-loathing is not virtue. War and destroying others is not a virtue; it is cowardice. We no longer have the luxury to argue the moral validity of this or that war. The destructive capacity of our world is so enormous that it overwhelms the combined destructive capacity of humankind throughout time. Those acts are acts of the ego, not of rational long-term thought, and not of the heart. What our world needs now is heart. So many people around the world are finally waking up and embracing a new kind of thinking and enlightened perspective—this is no accident. It's a larger force's way of pleading for survival.

Yes, risk and change often bring pain, but if we are willing to risk, walk through fire, face and embrace all of who and what we are and have been in order to reach a more authentic place within ourselves, we will quickly find a world beginning to heal. When we make choices from fear, we ultimately attract that which we are afraid of. Oddly it works the opposite from our intention. What you focus on expands. What will you choose to focus on?

In this choice between love and fear, I am committed to choosing love. Love and respect of self, of others, and of this planet. I prefer embracing life's challenges in an effort to be true to myself. I prefer the pursuit of a greater vision to the perceived safety of mere existence. It begins with self-love. I invite you to join me in choosing love.

I leave you with these words from Deepak Chopra's *The Seven Spiritual Laws of Success*:

"Attention energizes, and intention transforms. Whatever you put your attention on will grow stronger in your life. Whatever you take your attention away from will wither, disintegrate, and disappear. Intention, on the other hand, triggers transformation of energy and information...The quality of intention on the object of attention will orchestrate an infinity of space-time events to bring about the outcome intended, provided one follows the other spiritual laws of success."

Final Reflections:

1. *What do you believe you can do that will make a positive difference in someone's life? Are you willing to do that?*

2. *What are you most afraid of that someone will find out about you? Is it true? If so, then what will happen if they do find out? Why does it matter? How does this affect you on a daily basis, in what you say or how you behave? What can you do to eliminate this fear from your life?*

3. *Do you know someone who is in denial about something? How does it impact their behavior? What do you think of that? Are you in denial about something?*

4. *How do you show self-love?*

5. *Think of something in nature that you enjoy such as a beautiful sunset or sunrise, flowers, the ocean or lake, hiking, or anything else that speaks to you. How can you show your appreciation to the earth for these things?*

6. *List some actions you can take to become more self-aware and stay connected with your inner self.*

7. *Describe your highest vision of yourself. What is your intention towards that vision?*

8. *If you were to die tomorrow, what would you wish you had done in your life? What are you going to do about it?*

ACKNOWLDEGMENTS

This book could not have happened without my team of life's champions and wizards. You are my friends, family and innovators who embody the best the world has to offer. I love each and every one of you. Who you are along with your love, support, insights, efforts and inspirations are valuable beyond measure. You have my everlasting gratitude. You know who you are.

Made in the USA
Monee, IL
07 July 2026

56550092R00095